NOT WITHOUT A SCAR

CHOICES AND CONSEQUENCES

LAWRENCE OJI

COVENANT PUBLISHING

Not Without A Scar: Choices And Consequences
Lawrence Oji

Unless otherwise stated, all scripture quotations are taken from the Holy Bible, New King James Version (NKJV). Other versions cited are NIV, KJV, GNB, God's Word, MSG, LEB and NLT.

ISBN 978-1-907734-37-3
First Edition, First Printing September 2018

For permission requests, write to the publisher, addressed "Attention: Permission Coordinator" at the email address below:

Covenant Publishing
samadewunmi@btinternet.com

Cover Design by Covenant Publishing Team
Published by Covenant Publishing
Printed in the United Kingdom

TABLE OF CONTENTS

Endorsements

I am privileged once again to be asked to write a few words on behalf of our Evangelist and Pastor Evang. Lawrence Oji. He has demonstrated again, an exemplary ability to weave his personal life, his various trials, tests and eventual testimonies into a book. I have always believed that a man that shares a more profound testimony is one who went through test and comes out better and points the credit to God. It makes any writing or revelation from such a person truly erudite and deep. This book touched on many things, but I truly enjoy reading the times Pastor Solution tried to end his life, but every attempt was frustrated by divine design. It shows that if you are not the owner or creator of a thing, you cannot end or destroy it. Pride in man makes us believe we can seek greater things beyond what God has given us. No wonder, once we realise we cannot get it, greater pride leads us to see life as unsatisfactory. C.S. Lewis described pride in Mere Christianity. He says "Pride gets no pleasure out of having something, only out of having more of it than the next man. It is the comparison that makes you proud: the pleasure of being above the rest. Once the element of competition is gone, pride is gone." Let us take that negative competitive lust out of our life, and all will be well. I am wholly grateful to have to read this book and to endorse it.

Rev. Tayo Arowojolu
New Covenant Church
Edmonton Conference Pastor

Dedication

I have imagined continuously what my life would have been like by now after I lived for so long on drugs and my life seemed to have concluded even before starting.

Years spent on drugs and prisons with several accompanying suicide attempts had left scars on me to the point that I had resigned my fate to just being a loner even after I met Jesus Christ through Michael in that jail in Caltanissetta, Italy in April 2001.

Meeting Jesus restored the hope of living and destroyed that constant urge to end my life, even though the scars seemed not to have gone away. I was full of them and was regularly seeing them. To me it looked like the story I had read of Mephibosheth who remained lame in both legs even after David brought him from Lo Debar to the palace (2 Samuel 9:13), but God still had better plans ahead. He had preserved a STAR to bring out the testimonies in those scars of mine.

My meeting and marrying Stella-Maris, my shining STAR, meant my scars were turned to stars too. She chose not to look at those scars my past choices had left on me, but she instead chose to look at the stars in me the enemy had tried to cover (Job 37:21).

I dedicate this book to you, STAR BABY, my Angel, and my Shining Stainless Star.

I GENUINELY love you, and I pray that the Lord will reward you ABUNDANTLY and early in Jesus name.

You make my day EVERYDAY!

Acknowledgements

First of all, I want to say a very Big Thank You to the Lord who did not allow the wrong choices I made several years ago to destroy me. I had friends who went through the same path with me but didn't live to share their testimonies. It is all by His Grace that I survived.

I thank my General Overseer, Rev. Dr Paul Jinadu for taking time out of his hectic schedule to write the foreword to this book.

Special thanks to my Conference Pastor, Rev. Tayo Arowojolu for writing the Endorsement.

I thank you Sister Amy Ekwegh for proofreading the book for me.

Finally, Special thanks to God for ordering my steps to a wonderful woman, I call SSSS, Sweet Stainless Star Stella-Maris, my Apple, for not looking at the many scars my earlier choices in life left on me, and married me. I pray that the Lord will reward you plentifully and satisfy you early in Jesus mighty name. I thank you for always nudging me to see what the

Lord has deposited in me rather than concentrate on the scars my past choices left on me as the future is brighter. You always remind me that God couldn't have saved me to abandon me and that I will never have a better yesterday. Thank you my darling. I love you.

Foreword

When I was asked to write a foreword for this book, I did not know quite where to begin, for there's a lot I could say about the author. So I decided to start with a couple of quotes from this book.

"It is okay for you to define a mistake, but don't let a mistake define you."

"For instance, the decision to hang out with my marijuana-loving uncle meant that he succeeded in negatively influencing me. He initiated me into smoking of weeds and cigarettes which was to define my adolescent years."

As a result of wasted years students who were "less than average" overtook him. "While my younger ones become grandparents," he continues, "I am just starting off with bearing children."

These scars are real.

No one alive today has ever seen Jesus in the flesh. But when the redeemed of the Lord reach heaven, we will quite easily recognise Him; the scars of crucifixion. God alone can turn our Friday into a Good Friday. For in His hands our scars can become stars.

Of course, not all scars are visible. There are many walking wounded among us who cannot explain life's complexity. There are more questions than answers. Many adapt and stop looking for solutions. But, Praise God, there are solutions and healing in Christ, particularly inner healing, where it is needed most.

One man's experience and journey into life can be a good pointer to ways to gradual and wholesome recovery. I commend this book by my good disciple: Oji Lawrence (SOLUTION)

Rev. Dr. Paul Jinadu
General Overseer
New Covenant Church, Worldwide

Preface

Choices are crucial in life. Whether getting a spouse, a job, or anything material. Jesus said that whoever intends to build a house will sit down first and count the cost whether he has enough to finish it. That in itself means that the person will first know what type of house he needs to build. Some people can buy a car based on the price displayed, without first considering that the fuel consumption and the insurance would also affect their budget. It is not every "Buy now Pay later" you see that you must consider. It may look harmless at first, but ultimately the cost at the end may not be worthwhile.

One Pastor said that when he first came to the UK, he saw an offer to buy sofas and make the first payment six months later. He thought it was a good bargain and went for it. One day, after bringing in the sofas, his two sons were watching a cartoon on Kung-Fu and started practising what they watched on the sofas. By the time he started paying for the sofas, it was as though he was throwing money away because they were not worth the initial price as the boys had damaged most of the sofas.

A big house will also attract a fat Council Tax, and more gas to keep the house warm in winter.

All I am saying is that many things may need to be considered before deciding as choices are bound to leave marks, some of which cannot be wiped away.

I made my choices, and I am still paying the price for some of them several years after.

I pray that the Lord will open our eyes to His teachings and standards and guide us in making wise choices and decisions in life that will carry us along the journey of life. The Bible says in Psalm 11:3,

> *"If the foundations are destroyed, what can the righteous do?"*

If we get the foundation (choices) right then what we build (our future) will be stable, but if we do not, the future will be full of thorns. May the Spirit of God guide us into all truth as we allow Him to lead us in Jesus name. Only the Bible teaches the right path in life as we listen to what the Spirit says.

Chapter One
INTRODUCTION

Growing up in the sixties in Eastern Nigeria was fun. Aside from the Nigerian civil war which took place between 1967 and 1970, I had a fascinating childhood with loving parents. My father, Oji Kanu was in the Government Service! He was one of the few people at that time to work with the Colonial masters popularly referred to as the 'White Man'. This position was highly respected and revered! He was prosperous, and highly commended for his hard work.

Compared to other children living in our native town of Arochukwu, I had everything. We were housed in the government quarters in the Northern part of Nigeria – Kano precisely. The quarters were very comfortable. We had a sitting room and two bedrooms, our kitchen and bathroom, situated in a well-planned estate with around fifteen other families in houses of identical design. I had a bicycle, which I rode around the estate and a giant red ball. This sticks in my memory because I was the only child to have these things to play with. I was even more privileged compared with children from my wider hometown.

I can, therefore, say that I was born with the proverbial silver spoon in my mouth. In addition, I was a very promising child. The kind of child every mother wished for: kind, caring, honest, bright, and hardworking. I could have risen to the top echelons of life in my native Nigeria through the civil service, the Military or the private sector. I could have been anything I wanted.

In fact, everyone thought I had it all, but one singular decision was to change the course of my life forever. It took just one decision to change it all. Yes, the single decision to start smoking cigarette changed the entire trajectory of my life for the worse.

A loving uncle – my favourite at the time in a bid to show me how much he loved me introduced me to his passion for marijuana. As a young boy, I used to hang out with him in his 'joint'. I will normally watch him roll his marijuana cigarettes in blue writing paper. While I sat with him, watching him roll them, he gave me a puff or two. The weed was so strong and potent that it sent me sky high, and I would go home afterwards feeling extremely tired and hungry.

However, I kept returning for more because I loved the 'rush' I felt after each puff. At that time, I did not realise I was starting an addiction.

It started very innocently! From smoking a stick of cigarette to smoking marijuana, then crack and drug trafficking. Of course, the decision came with its consequences of perpetual prison terms ultimately leading to almost 40 years of wasted life.

Such is the power of decision. Whatever decision we take in life has a consequence. Each decision leaves a scar. Each scar tells a story. The story can be either positive or negative. I pray your scar tells a positive story because mine does not particularly tell a positive story in the beginning until I embraced Christ.

Looking back now over the years of waste; precious years that can never be recovered, I feel compelled to write this book – NOT WITHOUT A SCAR to emphasise the importance of the decisions we make in life.

The objective is to make people understand that there will be consequences to any decision we make. Sometimes these can be unpredictable and unexpected. The primary focus here is on a decision that you clearly know is bad! My definition of a wrong decision is one in which you damn the consequences and choose an option you know you should not.

Though life is full of choices, there are consequences – positive or negative. In economics, it is called "Opportunity Cost."

In the words of J.E.B. Spreadmann in his book, An Unforgivable Secret, 'Choices made, whether bad or good, follow you forever and affect everyone in their path one way or another."

Chapter Two
SCARS

*"There is a way that appears to be right, but
in the end, it leads to death" (Proverbs 14:12).*

As recounted in my Introduction and my first book, 'From Prison to Pulpit', I lived a life of waste: a life of drug addiction and perpetual imprisonment for nearly 40 years.

Between prison, smoking and drug-peddling, I felt I did not have much to live for. I had no friends, no wife and no children. My life was an empty cycle of punishment and self-harm. I was fed up with life and desperately wanted to end it all. I suffered years of depression and attempted suicide several times.

One instance stood out! I was going through a protracted period of depression at the time and went completely insane after a minor argument with the lady I just married barely three months previously. In an uncontrollable rage, I swallowed whole bottles of pills and painkillers on sight. I grabbed a knife and plunged it into my stomach, hoping to bleed to death. I fell to the floor and passed out of consciousness. Fortunately, the police found me and rushed me to the hospital where the medical staff fought to save my life. When I woke up at the hospital, the knife-wound had been stitched up, but I would be forever left with an ugly, jagged scar to remind me of the unwise decision I took at the time.

Any decision or any action a man takes in the course his life's journey has a consequence. It is therefore absolutely important to think things through before embarking on any trip. As a Pastor friend of mine aptly puts it, "Life is not a dress rehearsal. This is it". There is only one lifetime.

Another friend said that what we are experiencing today is the fruit of a seed planted yesterday. There is a payday for everyone. Whatever a man does today will affect his future either positively or negatively. In other words, whatever action one takes today will inevitably leave a mark. That mark is what I chose to describe as a scar.

That brings us to the critical question – what is a scar? There are various definitions of a scar, but I will give just a few of those.

A scar is a mark left by a healed wound, sore or burn. The Bible states clearly that Jesus's wounds left scars on His body, as evidence of what He went through on the Cross for us. "Now Thomas, called the Twin, one of the twelve, was not with them when Jesus came. The other disciples, therefore, said to him, "We have seen the Lord." So he said to them, "Unless I see in His hands the print of the nails, and put my finger into the print of the nails, and put my hand into His side, I will not believe." (John 20:24-25). Thomas was talking about the scars on Jesus as a consequence of the wounds that He sustained during the beatings and crucifixion. These scars are physical.

A scar is a lasting after-effect of trouble, especially a lasting psychological injury resulting from suffering or trauma.

In another definition, a scar could be described as a mark indicating a former point of attachment, as where a leaf has fallen from a stem.

A scar is an indelible mark a mistake leaves as a reminder of that mistake. This can be called an emotional scar. The definition of a mistake is an incorrect act or decision. We all make them. We all find ourselves on the hurt end of a mistake. We all have wished that at some point we had a redo to erase a particular act or decision. Remember it is okay for you to define a mistake, but don't let a mistake define you. I will write more in-depth on this in subsequent chapters of this book.

The scar I am referring to in this write-up is not necessarily a physical one. For instance, the decision to hang out with my marijuana-loving uncle meant that he succeeded in influencing me in a negative manner. He initiated me into smoking of weeds and cigarettes which was to define my adolescent years. Even though I was a very brilliant student, the love and time I dedicated to frivolous lifestyle meant that I allowed students who were less than average overtake me as other things took my interest rather than the real deal. Several years later I am still suffering from the scar. During the wasted years, my age mates and contemporaries overtook me in almost all aspects of life. For instance, while my younger siblings have all become grandparents, I am just starting off with having children. At the time of writing this book, my first child is only nine years old! This simply buttresses the saying that, "Time waits for no one."

Everyone alive has only twenty-four hours in a day, but what makes the difference is how each person chooses to invest his or her own. My prayer is that the Lord will give us the grace and the wisdom to know how to invest our time in positive things and not waste it. One can lose money and get another opportunity to make money, whereas time spent unwisely is gone for good.

I wasted my teenage years on drugs and prisons where I was always in and out due to my addiction to and dealings on drugs. My life was a real waste at the time to the extent that I did not have any interest in how I lived or died. It is only because of God's grace that I am alive today, yet there are obvious consequences as a result of the decisions I made then. My story will be incomplete unless someone adds, "Ex-drug addict and a jailbird". I am still suffering uncountable negative consequences even though I have been 'cleaned up' since 21 March 2001.

A couple of years ago, I had an invitation to minister in the United States of America. Surprisingly, I was refused a visa because of my past dealings with drugs. I bless the name of the Lord for giving me a great wife in Stella, even though many people tried to discourage her from marrying me because of my past experiences with hard drugs and all purportedly after I was free from drugs and embraced a new life in Christ Jesus. Some people could still not see beyond the drug addiction tag.

This is what scars represent. Long after the rocket has passed, it still leaves a considerable smoke in its trail. Therefore, we need to ensure that we make the right decisions in life because we have only this one life to live! Life is not a dress rehearsal.

There are always guiding rules and principles that would determine if one would achieve desired goals for whatever one does and unless these principles are observed to the letter the expected results may remain an illusion. For instance, in the game of football, a player is penalised for handling the ball rather than kicking the ball depending on what area of the pitch the foul is committed. However, if the player handled the ball within his penalty area of the pitch, a penalty would be awarded against his team, in which case it is sheer luck for a goal not to be conceded from the resulting penalty kick. If on the other hand, the player who committed the penalty happens to be the "last man" and there was a clear occasion of goal, that player would be sent off and his team reduced by one. In the 2010 World Cup Quarter Finals match between Uruguay and Ghana, Luis Suarez handled the ball on the goal line to prevent Ghana from scoring what would have been the winning goal and send the latter into the Semi-Finals. Suarez was given a red card, leaving his team a player less, while Asamoah Gyan missed the resulting penalty, making it impossible for Ghana to qualify thereby failing to make history as the first African nation to feature in a World Cup Semifinal. Both incidents left scars that will never go away. Therefore, it is important to understand that there is always a repercussion or consequence for every decision we take in life.

SCARS LEAVE INDELIBLE MARKS

I often hear Christians who undoubtedly embark on a wrong path say God's grace is sufficient. Of course, our God is merciful and full of grace, but He is also a consuming fire.

Everything we do as far as our walk with and our work for God are concerned must be in line with His own specified standard.

So many people have chosen to serve God their "own" way rather than His way, forgetting that it is either His way or No way. This is the truth that most people will not be willing to hear but need to be told.

Hurting someone with the truth is better than making them happy with a lie. It is needful to remember always that nothing gives God greater joy than to see that His people walk in the truth (3 John 4).

A very dear Pastor friend of mine, once said, "There are so many pew 'warmers' in the church because there are few 'warners' in the pulpit."

"True Christians rebuke sin and expose it. False Christians practice sin and defend it with "God will understand.""

While some scars can be wiped away over time, some others are indelible.

There are several instances in the Bible that supports this statement. In 2 Samuel 9, the Bible shows that even after King David had restored Mephibosheth (who was King Saul's grandson and son to Jonathan), given him back everything his grandfather, Saul, owned, made him sit at the same table to dine with him; he remained lame on his feet. Though the lameness was not due to a lame decision taken by Mephibosheth, yet the scar remained with him for life.

Galatians also talks about a scar on one's life. Galatians 6:17 says,

> "From henceforth let no one trouble me because I have upon me the mark of our Lord, Jesus Christ."

The mark there represents a scar.

Scars are meant to be indelible, that means nothing can remove them. They can be good scars, and there can also be bad or negative scars. I pray that ours will always be positive scars in Jesus name.

Chapter Three
CHOICES AND CONSEQUENCES

I suppose the big question would then be, "How do we make the right choices?" My answer lies in the Word of God. What are those things that we have allowed into our lives that will ultimately lead us to the wrong path? The devil who has only one assignment which is to steal, destroy and kill has several weapons that he employs to ensure that negative scars are inflicted on us. I will be addressing some of the common ones in this chapter.

OBEDIENCE IS KEY

God desires that we may faithfully serve our generation according to His own perfect will (Acts 13:36). This we can achieve by observing what is written in 2 Peter 1:1-11:

> *"Simon Peter, a bondservant and Apostle of Jesus Christ, to those who have obtained like precious faith with us by the righteousness of*

our God and Saviour Jesus Christ: Grace and peace be multiplied to you in the knowledge of God and of Jesus our Lord, as His divine power has given to us all things that pertain to life and godliness, through the knowledge of Him who called us by glory and virtue, by which have been given to us exceedingly great and precious promises, that through these you may be partakers of the divine nature, having escaped the corruption that is in the world through lust. But also, for this reason, giving all diligence, add to your faith virtue, to virtue knowledge, to knowledge self-control perseverance, to perseverance godliness, to godliness brotherly kindness, and to brotherly kindness love. For if these things are yours and abound, you will be neither barren nor unfruitful in the knowledge of our Lord Jesus Christ. For he who lacks these things is short-sighted, even to blindness, and has forgotten that he was cleansed from his old sins. Therefore brethren, be even more diligent to make your call and election sure, for if you do these things, you will never stumble, for so an entrance will be supplied to you abundantly into the everlasting kingdom of our Lord and Saviour Jesus Christ."

God wants us to obey Him in all things. To Him, that is the proof of our love for Him. In John 14:15, Jesus said:

"If you love Me, keep My commandments."

In John 15:14, He also said:

"You are My friends if you do whatever I command."

He learnt obedience Himself. Hebrews 5:8 says that,

"Though He was a Son, yet He learnt obedience from the things He suffered."

This means that whatever one suffers should teach them obedience. After all, the Bible states that:

"To obey is better than sacrifice, and to heed is better than the fat of rams" (1 Samuel 15:22).

There is always a consequence anytime we disobey God's commandment. Even in our obedience to His command, it is also vital to ensure that our motive is right. For instance, giving to God because we expect to get back from Him is a wrong motive. It is better to give offering because we love God who gave His Son because He loves us.

It is very pertinent to know that motive is everything. What is the motive behind your actions? It does not matter what one says or does! God is only interested in your heart motive.

People can be replaced for not obeying God's command to the letters. The motive is always what determines the outcome. Our motives are constantly in check. Some Christians are faithful while some others are "faceful." The faithful do what they ought to do whether the Pastor is watching them or not, whereas the "faceful" do what they do only when the Pastor or others are in view. God is not happy with unfaithful servants.

In 2 Kings 12:1-16, the King had commanded that contributions be taken so that the dilapidated Temple would be repaired, and instructed the priests to carry out the assignment, but when he found out after several years that the repairs to the Temple were not carried out, he replaced the priests with ordinary men without titles who then carried out the repairs of the Temple. It did not matter that they bore the title of priests, they got replaced. In Luke 19:40, Jesus made it clear that even stones can be used to replace those who fail in their required and privileged duty of praising God. May you not be replaced by anyone or even by a stone in Jesus name.

With God, half obedience is considered as disobedience. James 2:10 says,

> *"For whoever shall keep the whole law, and yet stumble in one point, he is guilty of all."*

There is always a consequence for every failure to carry out any of God's commands according to how He wants it done. There are certain things in the Word of God that are not mere suggestions but commands from the Master Himself. For example; the command to love your neighbour (John 13:34-35), and the command to Go and evangelise and tell the world that Jesus is alive and that He is the Lord (Matthew 28:1-20 and (Mark 16:7-8, 15-20) should also be considered as an act of disobedience if anyone refuse to obey fully to the letters. Jesus calls such a person, WICKED and LAZY for not carrying out those commands (Matthew 25:26). What a serious thing.

If we will not willingly go out and evangelise to souls living and dying without Christ, it means that we are not obedient servants and the consequence of that is that their blood will be on our heads.

Matthew 25:26 says,

> *"But his lord answered and said to him, you wicked and lazy servant, you knew that I reap where I have not sown and gather where I have not scattered seed."*

Anyone who loves what God hates is an enemy to God. God loves souls while the devil hates them. Satan puts people in prison whereas God sent His Son Jesus, to earth to release them. Isaiah 14:12-17 makes it clear that Satan puts men in prison, whereas Luke 4:18, Isaiah 10:38 and 1 John 3:8 demonstrates clearly what Jesus came to do here on earth - to set at liberty all those Satan put in bondage.

The Scriptures make it very clear too that after Jesus reconciled us to God through His sacrifice on the Cross, He also gave unto us the ministry of reconciliation that we may direct the lost back to God. We should do this work while it is day because no one can work in the night (John 9:4). Jesus says that He is the Light of the world, and in Matthew 5:14, He calls us the light of the world too. He says that the same work He did we will also do because He has given us power and authority to do exactly what He came to the world to do. He did not come to condemn but to save. He said,

> "AS my Father has sent Me I send you" (John 20:21).

We are to love what God loves and hate what He hates. Otherwise, we do not love Him. He said we should feed His sheep if we love Him. This means that those who starve His sheep, do not love Him.

James says,

> "You are like an unfaithful wife who loves her husband's enemies. Don't you realise that

*making friends with God's enemies; the evil
pleasures of this world, makes you an enemy of
God? I say it again, that if you aim to enjoy the
sinful pleasure of the unsaved world, you
cannot also be a friend of God (James 4:4,
TLB).*

Everyone likes to hear Good News. I firmly believe
that even a confirmed sadist would not mind
receiving good news. God Himself looked at His
creation and said, "It is good." However, after the fall,
man lost his beautiful and enviable position of
enjoying fellowship with God. He became ugly and
filthy. He did not deserve to be in God's presence
anymore, but because of His eternal plans for man to
enjoy eternity in His presence, God sent His Son, Jesus
Christ to come and redeem man from his filth.

It is important to understand that just as
disobedience to God's command attracts a curse, there
are tremendous rewards in obedience to His
command.

*"Husbands love your wives, just as Christ also
loved the Church and gave Himself for her,
that He might sanctify and cleanse her with the
washing of water by the word, that He might
present her to Himself a glorious church, not
having spot or wrinkle or any such thing, but*

that she should be holy and without blemish (scar)" (Ephesians 5:25-27).

In other words, the only way Jesus can present the Church back to Himself is when there is no scar. Scars would disqualify anyone from entering heaven. Christ gave His life for humanity on the Cross because of love, but will only take those who are cleansed by the blood and the Word. The Word of God is meant to wash us as we hear and receive it.

A man who maltreats his wife is not wise. He is blocking the heavens over his head, and consequently, his prayers to God cannot go beyond the roof (1 Peter 3:7).

The Bible says in Proverbs that,

"There is a way that seems right unto a man, but the end thereof are the ways of death" (Proverbs 14:12; 16:25).

When a person sins, God can forgive them through Jesus Christ, but there often are still negative earthly consequences for them. A man or a woman who goes to bed with everyone they meet, may repent and be forgiven, but if they have contracted a disease in the process, like gonorrhea, syphilis, or HIV, they will still live with the consequences. That is the scar they have to live with; and what a scar that is.

Even in the New Testament, it is written,

> *"Be not deceived; God is not mocked. Whatever a man sows that shall he also reap" (Galatians 6:7).*

Our service to God must be according to His standard and not our own. For instance, it is written in Matthew 15:7-9,

> *"Ye hypocrites, well did Esaias prophesy of you saying, "This people draweth nigh unto Me with their mouth, and honoureth Me with their lips, but their heart is far from Me. But in vain they do worship Me, teaching for doctrines the commandments of men.""*

Our service must be total; devoid of any form of hypocrisy.

Addressing hypocrisy, Apostle Paul says in Galatians 2:11-13,

> *"Now when Peter had come to Antioch, I withstood him to his face, because he was to be blamed; for before certain men came from James, he would eat with the Gentiles; but when they came, he withdrew and separated himself, fearing those who were of the circumcision. And the rest of the Jews also played the hypocrite with him, so that even Barnabas was carried away with their hypocrisy."*

This is emphasised in a number of scriptures:

Numbers 14:20-24 (MSG) says,

> "I forgive them, honouring your words. But as
> I live and as the glory of God fills the whole
> earth—not a single person of those who saw
> my glory, saw the miraculous signs I did in
> Egypt and the wilderness, and who have tested
> me over and over again, turning a deaf ear to
> me—not one of them will set eyes on the land
> I so solemnly promised to their ancestors. No
> one who has treated me with such repeated
> contempt will see it. But my servant Caleb—
> this is a different story. He has a different
> spirit; he follows me passionately. I'll bring
> him into the land that he scouted, and his
> children will inherit it."

In Numbers 14:26-30, God spoke to Moses and
Aaron saying,

> "How long is this going to go on, all this
> grumbling against me by this evil-infested
> community? I've had my fill of complaints
> from these grumbling Israelites. Tell them, As
> I live – God's decree - here is what I am going
> to do: Your corpses are going to litter the
> wilderness of you twenty years and older who
> were counted in the census, this whole
> generation of grumblers and grousers. Not one
> of you will enter the land and make your home

there, the firmly and solemnly promised land, except Caleb, son of Jephunneh and Joshua son of Nun."

A scar will appear at any point of detachment of a branch from the tree. Similarly, if after faithfully following the Lord, one allows himself to get detached from Him, a noticeable scar will be the result too. It is inevitable because there is always a consequence for every action or decision made.

Some great ministers of the Gospel were said to have gone to hell after preaching some powerful messages because of some wrong decisions they made during their earthly journey. They got detached from the Vine without knowing it, and that detachment left a scar that defined the latter part of their life and ministry.

Little wonder Paul said,

"I am careful about my flesh so that after I must have preached to others and brought them to salvation, I myself shall not be a castaway" (1 Corinthians 9:27).

This means it is possible to preach the Gospel to others and still not make heaven.

2 Chronicles 36:15-17 says,

> *"And the Lord God of their fathers sent warnings to them by His messengers, rising up early and sending them, because He had compassion on His people and on His dwelling place. But they locked the messengers of God, despised His words, and scoffed at His prophets, until the wrath of the Lord arose against His people, till there was no remedy. Therefore He brought against them the king of the Chaldeans, who killed their young men with the sword in the house of their sanctuary, and had no compassion on young man or virgin, on the aged or the weak; He gave them all into his hand."*

Whatever decision anyone makes in life to detach from God even if momentarily, leaves a scar. God wants to be obeyed, and He wants us to obey Him willingly too. In Isaiah 1:19, the Bible says, "If you are willing and obedient, you shall eat the good of the land.

1 Chronicles 29:9 says,

> *"Then the people rejoiced, for they had offered willingly because with a loyal heart they had offered willingly to the Lord; and King David also rejoiced greatly."*

Our obedience to God must be with a willing heart just as our giving Him of our service and worship must be of a willing heart too. Anything short of that is not good enough for our King.

Our obedience to God matters so much to Him than any sacrifice we may bring to Him. It is written in 1 Samuel 15:22 that obedience is better than sacrifice.

God always looks at our heart at all times. In fact, God said to Samuel whom He had sent to the house of Jesse to anoint a king to replace Saul,

> *"Do not look at his appearance or at his physical stature, because I have refused him. For the Lord does not see as man sees, for man looks at the outward appearance but the Lord looks at the heart" (1 Samuel 16:7).*

It does not matter how smartly we pretend, the Lord sees our hearts and judges our motives, and that is what determines how well or not a man will finish the race.

Jesus says,

> *"Hypocrites! Well did Isaiah prophesy about you, saying: These people draw near to Me with their mouth and honour Me with their lips, But their heart is far from Me, Teaching as doctrines the commandments of men" (Mark 7:6-7).*

"My heart within Me is broken because of the Prophets; All My bones shake. I am a drunken man, and like a man whom wine has overcome, Because of the Lord, and because of His holy words. For the land is full of adulterers; for because of a curse the land mourns. The pleasant places of the wilderness are dried up. Their course of life is evil, and their might is not right. For both prophet and priest are profane; Yes in My house I have found their wickedness, says the Lord. Therefore their way shall be to them like slippery ways; in the darkness, they shall be driven on and fall in them, the year of their punishment says the Lord. And I have seen folly in prophets of Samaria: They prophesied by Baal and caused My people Israel to err. Also, I have seen a horrible thing in the prophets of Jerusalem: They commit adultery and walk in lies; they also strengthen the hands of evildoers, So that no one turns back from his wickedness. All of them are like Sodom to Me, and their inhabitants like Gomorrah. Therefore thus says the Lord of hosts concerning the prophets: Behold, I will feed them with wormwood, and make them drink the water of gall; For from the Prophets of Jerusalem Profaneness has gone out into all the land. Thus says the Lord of hosts: Do not listen to the words of the prophets who prophesy to you. They make you worthless; They speak a vision of their own *heart, not from the mouth of the Lord. They continually say to those who despise Me, "The Lord has said, "You shall have peace"; and to anyone who walks according to the dictates of his own heart, they say, "No evil shall come upon you." For who has stood in the counsel of the Lord, and has perceived and heard His word? Who has marked His word and heard it? Behold a whirlwind of the Lord has gone forth in a fury – a violent whirlwind! It will fall violently on the head of the wicked. The anger of the Lord will not turn back until He has executed and performed the thoughts of His heart. In the latter days, you will understand it perfectly. I have not sent these prophets, yet they ran. I have not spoken to them, yet they prophesied. But if they had stood in My counsel, and had caused My people to hear My words, then they would have turned them from their evil way and from the evil of their doings. Am I a God near at hand, says the Lord, and not a God afar off? Can anyone hide himself in secret places, so I shall not see him? Says the Lord; Do I not fill heaven and earth? Says the Lord. I have heard what the prophets have said who prophesy lies in My name, saying, I have dreamed, I have dreamed! How long will this be in the heart of the prophets who prophesy lies? Indeed they are prophets of the deceit of their own heart, who try to make My people forget My name by their dreams which everyone tells his neighbour, as their fathers forget My name for Baal. The prophet who has a dream, let him tell a dream; and he who has My word, let him speak My word faithfully. What is the chaff to the wheat? Says the Lord. Is not My word like a fire? Says the Lord. And like a hammer that breaks the rock in pieces? Therefore behold, I am against the prophets, says the Lord, who steal My words everyone from his neighbour. Behold, I am against the prophets, says the Lord, who use their tongues and say, He says. Behold, I am against those who prophesy false dreams, says the Lord, and tell them, and cause My people to err by their lies and by their recklessness. Yet I did not send them or command them; therefore they shall not profit this people at all, says the Lord"* (Jeremiah 23:9-32).

In verse 33 the Lord says He will forsake such prophets. Yet that does not mean they could not be addressed by the title of prophets.

Ecclesiastes 9:8 says,

"Let thy garments be always white, and let thy head lack no ointment."

From the above, we can deduce that what matters is our continuity. In Daniel 6:16 and 6:20, the king spoke to Daniel about his God whom he served continually. The garment of service to God has to be continually white, else a scar would appear, and a negative scar cannot enter heaven. Ephesians 5:27 says,

> *"That He might present her to Himself a glorious church, not having spot or wrinkle or any such thing, but that she should be holy without blemish."*

In other words, not having spot or wrinkle means, not having a scar. Matthew 24:13 says,

> *"But he who endures until the end shall be saved."*

The race is a marathon and not a sprint. Wherever anyone misses the mark is their choice and not God's will. God wants us to finish victoriously, so that like Paul said in 2 Timothy 4:7-8, we too can say,

> *"I have fought a good fight, I have finished the race, I have kept the faith. Finally, there is laid up for me the crown of righteousness, which the Lord, the righteous Judge, will give to me on that Day, and not to me only but also to all who have loved His appearing."*

1 Corinthians 10:19-24 (MSG) say,

> *"Do you see the difference? Sacrifices offered to idols are offered to nothing, for what's the idol but a nothing? Alternatively, worse than nothing, a minus, a demon! I do not want you*

to become part of something that reduces you to less than yourself. And you can't have it both ways, banqueting with the Master one day and slumming with demons the next. Besides, the Master won't put up with it. He wants us-all or nothing. Do you think you can get off with anything less? Looking at it one way, you could say, "Anything goes. Because of God's immense generosity and grace, we don't have to dissect and scrutinize every action to see if it will pass muster. But the point is not to just get by. We want to live well, but our foremost efforts should be to help others live well."

The above clearly shows that there are certain decisions we make in life that will reduce us, take us into the slum meant for the devil and his demons, and inevitably cause us to be less than the perfect will of God for us.

COMPLAINING AND MURMURING

Complaining and grumbling may look harmless, yet it was strong enough to stop a whole generation from entering the Promised Land! Not only that, they wandered in the wilderness for 40 years! 1 Corinthians 10:10 says they murmured and were destroyed by the destroyer.

Are you murmuring or complaining rather than focusing on God Who is the awesome Changer? Think twice, because what He was yesterday, He is still today and He will forever remain. He does not change. Our God does not change. Malachi 3:6 says,

> "I am God I do not change"

Hebrews 13:8 says,

> "Jesus Christ is the same yesterday, today and forever."

God takes obedience to His word seriously. Failure to comply spells terrible consequences.

The Bible tells us in Romans 3:23-24,

> "For all have sinned and fallen short of the glory of God, being justified freely by His grace through the redemption that is in Christ Jesus."

Romans 6:23 says,

> "For the wages of sin is death, but the gift of God is eternal life in Christ Jesus our Lord."

So, sin has a price. Sin will always leave a scar. It does not matter how long one has walked in obedience to the commandments of God, the day the person decides to go astray, and God will not be pleased. And of course, this comes with consequences.

Proverbs 6:27-35 (MSG) records,

> *"Can a man scoop a flame into his lap and not have his clothes catch on fire? Can he walk on hot coals and not blister his feet? So it is with the man who sleeps with another man's wife. He who embraces her will not go unpunished. Excuses might be found for a thief who steals because he is starving. But if he is caught, he must pay back seven times what he stole, even if he has to sell everything in his house. But the man who commits adultery is an utter fool, for he destroys himself. He will be wounded and disgraced. His shame will never be erased. For the woman's jealous husband will be furious, and he will show no mercy when he takes revenge. He will accept no compensation, nor be satisfied with a payoff of any size."*

From the scriptures above, we can easily understand that disobedience is a sin and of course sin leaves a permanent scar that cannot be erased.

Ezekiel 18:23-28 (MSG) says,

> *"Do you think I take any pleasure in the death of wicked men and women? Isn't it my pleasure that they turn around, no longer living wrong but living right – really living? The same thing goes for a good person who turns his back on an upright life and starts sinning, plunging into the same vile*

obscenities that the wicked person practices. Will this person live? I do not keep a list of all the things this person did right, like money in the bank he can draw on. Because of his defection, because he accumulates sin, he will die. Do I hear you saying, "That's not fair, God is not fair"? Listen, Israel. Am I not fair? You're the ones who aren't fair! If a good person turns away from his good life and takes up sinning, he will die for it. He will die for his own sin. Likewise, if a bad person turns away from his bad life and starts living a good life, a fair life, he will save his life. Because he faces up to all the wrongs he has committed and put them behind him, he will live, really live. He won't die."

Romans 6:1-2 says,

"What shall we say then? Shall we continue in sin that grace may abound? Certainly not! How shall we who died to sin live any longer in it?"

Disobedience and pride come with grave consequences which may be fatal. An example is the fall of Lucifer which is recorded in the bible.

LUCIFER

Lucifer was the first to lose his place in heaven even after having served God as the head of the worship team. About Lucifer who was an angel of God and the Choirmaster in heaven, we read:

> "How you are fallen from heaven, O Lucifer, son of the morning! How you are cut down to the ground, you who weakened the nations! For you have said in your heart: "I will ascend into heaven, I will exalt my throne above the stars of God: I will also sit on the mount of the congregation on the farthest sides of the north; I will ascend above the heights of the clouds, I will be like the Most High. Yet you shall be brought down to Sheol, to the lowest depths of the Pit. Those who see you will gaze at you, and consider you, saying: "Is this the man who made the earth tremble, who shook kingdoms, who made the world as a wilderness and destroyed its cities, who did not open the house of his Prisoners? All the kings of the nations, all of them, sleep in glory, everyone in his own house; But you are cast out of your grave, like an abominable branch, Like the garment of those who are slain, thrust with a sword, who go down to the stones of the pit, like a corpse trodden underfoot. You will not be joined with them in burial, because you have destroyed your land and slain your people. The brood of

evildoers shall never be named. Prepare slaughter for his children because of the iniquity of their fathers, lest they rise up and possess the land, and fill the face of the world with cities." For I will rise up against them, says the Lord of hosts, and cut off from Babylon the name and remnant, and offspring and posterity, says the Lord. I will also make it a possession for the porcupine, and marshes of muddy water; I will sweep it with the broom of destruction, says the Lord of hosts, and cut off from Babylon the name and remnant, and offspring and posterity, says the Lord. I will also make it a possession for the porcupine, and marshes of muddy water; I will sweep it with the broom of destruction, says the Lord of hosts" (Isaiah 14:12-23).

This same account can be seen in Ezekiel 28:12-19,

"Son of man, take up a lamentation for the king of Tyre, and say to him, "Thus says the Lord God: You were the seal of perfection, Full of wisdom and perfect in beauty. You were in Eden, the garden of God; every precious stone was your covering: The Sardius, Topaz, and Diamond, Beryl, Onyx, and Jasper, Sapphire, Turquoise, and Emerald with Gold. The workmanship of your timbrels and pipes was prepared for you on the day you were created. You were the anointed cherub who covers; I established you; you were on the holy

mountain of God; you walked back and forth in the midst of fiery stones. You were perfect in your ways from the day you were created. Till iniquity was found in you. By the abundance of your trading, you became filled with violence within, and you sinned; therefore, I cast you as a profane thing out of the mountain of God; and I destroyed you, o covering cherub, from the midst of the fiery stones. Your heart was lifted up because of your beauty; you corrupted your wisdom for the sake of your splendour; I cast you to the ground, I laid you before kings that they might gaze at you. You defiled your sanctuaries by the multitude of your iniquities, by the iniquity of your trading; therefore, I brought fire from your midst; it devoured you to ashes upon the earth in the sight of all who saw you. All who knew you among the peoples are astonished at you; you became a horror, and shall be no more forever."

O how are the mighty fallen! And still capable of falling! As Christians, it is important that we constantly have a self-audit or evaluation to see if and where we may be missing the mark. The Apostle Paul in his writing to the Corinthians says,

"Examine yourselves, whether ye be in the faith; prove your own selves. Know ye, not your own selves, how that Jesus Christ is in

*you, except ye be reprobates?" (2 Corinthians
13:5, KJV).*

Every fall delays one's movement and prolongs the
journey. As one keeps falling and getting up, the one
who did not fall will have a higher probability of
getting to the destination first. I pray that we will not
fall short and lose our position in Jesus name.

GREED

Peter Tosh, the late Jamaican reggae musician in
one of his albums titled "Equal Rights", clearly warns
that peace on this planet earth will always remain an
illusion until there is equal right and justice, while the
late Jimi Hendrix, the American rock guitarist says,
"When the power of love overcomes the love of
power, the world will know Peace."

Only those who understand grace will know how
to show the REAL love which guarantees world peace.

One of the greatest weapons the enemy can use to
inflict a scar on a believer is the spirit of greed. Where
the spirit of greed is in operation, there can be no love
and therefore no peace.

The Bible says in Proverbs 15:16,

> *"Better is a little with the fear of the Lord than great treasure with trouble," and in Proverbs 16:8, "Better is a little righteousness, than vast revenues without justice."*

O how many people have confused the pursuit of gold as the pursuit of God.

Paul said in Philippians 3:7-8,

> *"But what things were gain to me, these I have counted loss for Christ. Yet indeed I also count all things loss for the excellence of the knowledge of Christ Jesus my Lord, for whom I have suffered the loss of all things, and count them as rubbish, that I may gain Christ."*

Verse 14 says,

> *"I press toward the goal for the prize of the upward call of God in Christ Jesus."*

A contented man cannot be tempted. Paul said in Philippians,

> *"I know how to abound and I know how to abase. I can do all things through Christ who strengthens me" (Philippians 4:12-13).*

What does the Bible say about greed?

Greed is a strong and selfish desire to have more of something - most often money or power. There are many warnings in the Bible about giving in to greed and longing for riches. Jesus warned,

> "Watch out! Be on your guard against all kinds of greed; a man's life does not consist in the abundance of his possession" (Luke 12:15).

> "Do not store up for yourselves treasures on earth, where moth and rust destroy and where thieves break in and steal. You cannot serve both God and money" (Matthew6:19, 24b).

Greed and desire for riches are traps that bring ruin and destruction. The love of money is a root of all kinds of evil, and Christians are warned.

> "Do not put your trust in wealth" (1 Timothy 6:9-10, 17-18).

Covetousness or having an excessive desire for more is IDOLATRY, and our God is a jealous God who alone wants to be worshipped.

Ephesians 5:5-6 says,

> "For this you know, that no fornicator, unclean person, nor covetous man, who is an IDOLATERS, has any inheritance in the kingdom of Christ and God. Let no one deceive you with empty words, for because of these

> *things the wrath of God comes upon the sons of disobedience. Therefore do not be partakers with them."*

Hebrews 13:5 says,

> *"Let your conduct be without covetousness; be content with such things as you have. For He Himself has said, "I will never leave you nor forsake you."*

It is the love of money or greed for money itself that is the problem. The love of money is a sin because it gets in the way of worshipping God genuinely. Jesus said it could be tough for rich people to enter the kingdom of God. When the rich young ruler asked Jesus what he should do to inherit eternal life, Jesus told him to sell all his possessions and give the money to the poor. When the young man heard this, he went away sad because he had great wealth (Matthew 19:16-22, Mark 10:17-27).

By instructing him to give up his money, Jesus pointed out the young man's main problem: GREED and the love of money. The man could not follow Christ because he was following money. His love of this world interfered with his love for God.

Greed refuses to be satisfied. More often, the more we get, the more we want. Material possessions will not protect us in this life or eternally. Jesus' parable of the Rich Fool in Luke 12:13-21 illustrates this point well. Also Psalm 49:10 makes it even more apparent too.

Again money or wealth is not the problem. The problem is our attitude towards money. When we place our confidence in wealth or are consumed by the insatiable desire for more, we are failing to give God the glory and worship He deserves. We are to serve God, not wasting our time pursuing wealth (Proverbs 23:4).

Our heart's desire should be to store up riches in heaven and not worry about what we will eat or drink or wear. But seek first the kingdom of God and His righteousness and all these things will be given to you as well (Matthew 6:25-34).

One notable example in the Bible of how greed can leave a perpetual scar on a generation is found in 2 Kings 5:20-27,

> *"But Gehazi, the servant of Elisha the man of God, said, "Look, my master has spared Naaman this Syrian, while not receiving from his hands what he brought; but as the Lord lives, I will run after him and take something from him." So Gehazi pursued Naaman. When Naaman saw him running after him, he got down from his chariot to meet him, and said, "Is all well?" And he said, "All is well. My*

*master has sent me, saying, "Indeed, just now
two young men of the sons of the prophets have
come to me from the mountains of Ephraim.
Please give them a talent of silver and two
changes of garments." So Naaman said,
"Please, take two talents." And he urged him,
and bound two talents of silver in two bags,
with two changes of garments, and handed
them to two of his servants; and they carried
them on ahead of him. When he came to the
Citadel, he took them from their hand, and
stored them away in the house; then he let them
go, and they departed. Now he went in and
stood before his master. Elisha said to him,
"Where did you go, Gehazi?" And he said,
"Your servant did not go anywhere." Then he
said to him, "Did not my heart go with you
when the man turned back from his chariot to
meet you? Is it time to receive money and to
receive clothing, olive groves and vineyards,
sheep and oxen, male and female servants?
Therefore the leprosy of Naaman shall cling to
you and your descendants forever." And he
went out from his presence leprous, as white as
snow."*

By His greed for money, Naaman left a legacy of
leprosy for his lineage. Unfortunately, most messages
one hears on the pulpits and television these days are
messages that make one believe that Jesus went to the
Cross solely because of money. Most of the time you

hear the Scripture "Money answereth all things", and they will quote Ecclesiastes. I ask if they ever read the Scripture in Acts of the Apostles 8:20 that says explicitly that there are things money cannot buy.

Often, many Pastors having delivered an excellent sermon will also allow the greed inside them to come out by manipulating their congregations, sometimes making them afraid with the way they will twist scriptures, so they are coerced into giving money. They will even use the Scriptures to back it up and say the Lord told them. They forget that those who allow the spirit of greed to direct them in ministry will also suffer spiritual leprosy that can go through their lineage as a legacy.

The eyes of God go to and fro all over the earth at any given time. Our motives are constantly in check. Nothing can be hidden from Him. Men of God should be careful and not be taken over by greed in ministry because everyone's work will be tested at the end. There is a Pay Day for everyone.

The Bible says clearly in Psalm 62:12,

> *"Also to You, O Lord, belongs mercy; For You render to each one according to his work."*

Also in Proverbs 11:18,

> *"The wicked man does deceptive work, but he who sows righteousness will have a sure reward."*

Brethren there is also a reward; a compensation for greed in ministry and it is not a palatable one. If you have been deceiving your congregation, you should repent and make restitution.

IMMORALITY

For example, Solomon was the King God allowed to build His Temple instead of his father, David. He asked for wisdom when God gave him an open cheque to ask for whatever he desired. He enjoyed a very privileged place with God. However, of him, the Bible records in Nehemiah 13:26,

> *"Did not Solomon King of Israel sin by these things? Yet among many nations was there no king like him, who was beloved of his God, and God made him king over all Israel: nevertheless, even him did outlandish women cause to sin."*

It did not matter that Solomon enjoyed a great privilege, it was still recorded that women caused him to sin and that sin caused him his enviable position with God.

1 John 2:16 says,

> *"For all that is in the world, the lust of the flesh, and the lust of the eyes, and the pride of life, is not of the Father but is of the world."*

There is need to be always on alert because the day of the Lord will come unannounced. That is why it is written in Mark 13:32-37,

> *"But of that day and that hour knoweth no man, no, not the angels which are in heaven, neither the Son, but the Father. Take ye heed, watch and pray: for ye know not when the time is. For the Son of Man is as a man taking a far journey, who left his house, and gave authority to his servants, and to every man his work, and commanded the porter to watch. Watch ye therefore: for ye know not when the Master of the house cometh, at evening or at midnight, or at the cockcrowing, or in the morning: Lest coming suddenly he finds you sleeping. And what I say unto you, I say unto all, watch."*

Revelations 16:15 also says,

> *"Behold I come as a thief. Blessed is he that watcheth, and keepeth his garments, lest he walk naked, and they see his shame."*

What these scriptures are emphasising is that it is possible to start well the walk with the Master and still miss the mark due to one disobedience or the other. The starting is not as important as the finishing. That is why the Scripture says,

> *"But the one who endures to the end will be saved" (Matthew 24:13).*

God says in Jeremiah 29:11,

> *"For I know the thoughts and plans I have for you, says the Lord, thoughts and plans for welfare and peace and not for evil, to give you hope in your final outcome."*

Psalms 139:17 says,

> *"How precious also are Your thoughts to me, O God! How great is the sum of them!"*

Jesus says that He came that we might have life and have it in abundance. Therefore, certain decisions we make in life can short-circuit God's perfect plan for us.

It is not God's will for anyone to end in hell because that place is where Satan the devil and his angels are (Matthew 25:41). Hellfire is where people go by choice, their own choice as a result of their disobedience to the voice of the Master.

God's will is that no one will end up in hell with Satan and his angels. He sent His only Son, Jesus to ensure that everyone will make heaven at the end of his or her sojourn here on earth, but He will not force anyone to go to heaven. In John 3:16, it is clearly stated that,

> *"Because God loved the world so much, He sent His Son Jesus to die on the Cross so that those who will believe in Him will not perish but have everlasting life."*

Jesus said that He had gone ahead to prepare a place for those who believe in Him so that they too will stay with Him in eternity (John 14:1-6).

It was never in God's plan to make anybody spend eternity in hellfire. People go there as a matter of their own choice.

Psalm 9:17 says,

> *"The wicked shall be turned into hell and all the nations that forget God."*

> *"Therefore hell hath enlarged herself, and opened her mouth without measure: and their glory, and their multitude, and their pomp, and he that rejoiceth shall descend into it. And the mean man shall be brought down, and the mighty man shall be humbled, and the eyes of the lofty shall be humbled: But the Lord of*

hosts shall be exalted in judgement, and God that is holy shall be sanctified in righteousness" (Isaiah 5:14-16).

"But when the righteous turns away from his righteousness, and commits iniquity, and does according to all the abominations that the wicked man does, shall he live? All his righteousness that he has done shall not be mentioned: in his trespass that he has trespassed, and in his sin that he has sinned, in them shall he die. Yet you say, The way of the Lord is not equal. Hear now, O house of Israel; Is not My way equal? Are not your ways unequal? When a righteous man turns away from his righteousness and commits iniquity, and dies in them, for the iniquity he has done shall he die" (Ezekiel 18:24-26).

"And the Lord said unto Moses, Whoever has sinned against Me, him will I blot out of My book" (Exodus 32:33).

It is imperative to repent once one realises they have gotten anything wrong with the Lord otherwise they will face the repercussion.

For instance, we read from Jeremiah 3:13-17 that,

"Only acknowledge thine iniquity, that thou hast transgressed against the Lord thy God, and has scattered thy ways to the strangers

under every green tree, and ye have not obeyed my voice, saith the Lord. Turn, O backsliding children, saith the Lord; for I am married unto you: and I will take you one of a city, and two of a family, and I will bring you to Zion. And I will give you Pastors according to my heart, which shall feed you with knowledge and understanding. And it shall come to pass, when ye be multiplied and increased in the land, in those days, saith the Lord, they shall say no more, "The ark of the covenant of the Lord:" neither shall they remember it; neither shall they visit it; neither shall that be done any more. At that time they shall call Jerusalem the throne of the Lord; and all the nations shall be gathered unto it, to the name of the Lord, to Jerusalem; neither shall they walk any more after the imagination of their evil heart."

This clearly shows that God gave Shepherds after His own that will direct the sheep on the right path to heaven to spend eternity with Jesus.

That is why He says to the Shepherds in Proverbs 27:23,

"Be thou diligent to know the state of thy flocks and look well to thy herds."

Unfortunately, there are Shepherds who have chosen to do their own business rather than do God's and still pretend to be doing God's business. To those shepherds the Lord says in Ezekiel 34:1-6,

> *"And the word of the Lord came unto me, saying, Son of man, prophesy against the shepherds of Israel, prophesy, and say unto them, "Thus saith the Lord God unto the shepherds; Woe be to the shepherds of Israel that do feed themselves! Should not the shepherds feed the flock? Ye eat the fats, and you clothe you with the wool, ye kill them that are fed: but ye feed not the flock. The diseased have ye not strengthened, neither have ye healed that which was sick, neither have ye bound up that which was broken, neither have ye brought again that which was driven away, neither have ye sought that which was lost; but with force and with cruelty have ye ruled them. And they were scattered, because there is no shepherd; and they became meat to all the beasts of the field, when they were scattered. My sheep wondered through all the mountains, and upon every high hill; yea, My flock was scattered upon all the face of the earth, and none did search or seek after them.""*

The Bible also has it boldly recorded in Deuteronomy 30:19-20,

> *"I call Heaven and Earth to witness against you today: I place before you Life and Death,*

Blessing and Curse. Choose life so that you and your children will live. And love God, your God, listening obediently to Him, firmly embracing Him. Oh yes, He is life itself, a long life settled on the soil that God, your God, promised to give your ancestors, Abraham, Isaac, and Jacob.''

Someone once said that the meaning of the word, BIBLE, is *'Believers Instructions Before Leaving Earth.'* This means that our Maker did not just make us and leave us without a manual of how to conduct our lives here on earth before leaving it.

Every word from God's mouth comes to pass. Let us look at what the Bible records in Ezekiel 23:22-30 following the disobedience of Oholibah.

"Therefore, Oholibah, thus says the Lord God: Behold I will stir up your lovers against you, from whom you have alienated yourself, and I will bring them against you from every side: The Babylonians, all the Chaldeans, Pekod, Shoa, Koa, all the Assyrians with them, all of them desirable young men, Governors and rulers, Captains and men of renown, all of them riding on horses. And they shall come against you with chariots, wagons, and war horses, with a horde of people. They shall array against you, buckler, shield, and helmet all around. I will delegate judgement to them, and

they shall judge you according to their judgements. I will set My jealousy against you, and they shall deal furiously with you; they shall remove your nose and your ears, and your remnant shall fall by the sword; they shall take your sons and your daughters, and your remnant shall be devoured by fire. They shall also strip you of your clothes and take away your beauty jewellery. Thus I will make you cease your lewdness and your harlotry brought from the land of Egypt so that you will not lift your eyes to them nor remember Egypt any more. For thus says the Lord God: Surely I will deliver you into the hand of those you hate, into the hand of those from whom you alienated yourself. They will deal hatefully with you, take away all you have worked for, and leave you naked and bare. The nakedness of your harlotry shall be uncovered, both your lewdness and your harlotry. I will do these things to you because you have gone as a harlot after the Gentiles; because you have become defiled by their idols."

Are you serving God with your eyes on other things other than God? What have you become defiled with while serving God? Do you have a divided interest while proclaiming that you are following God? Examine yourself because every fall will cause a wound that will leave a scar.

God's will is not for anyone to depreciate but to bear fruit.

In John 15:8 (AMPC), Jesus says,

> *"When you bear (produce) much fruit, My Father is honoured and glorified, and you show and prove yourselves to be true followers of Mine."*

God intends that we will be fulfilled according to His plans and patterns for us.

Chapter Four

PRIDE IS AN ENEMY

"God is stern in dealing with the arrogant, but to the humble, He shows kindness." (Proverbs 3:34, NAB).

Pride is a clothing people wear without even realising they are putting it on. It is something God abhors more than any other thing. Even so, humility also is a form of clothing. No wonder Paul says in Colossians 3:12,

"Since God chose you to be the holy people He loves, you must CLOTHE yourselves with kindness, HUMILITY, gentleness, and patience."

When I was a drug addict, nothing else mattered. Life was drugs. From rising in the morning until I retire for the day, only one thought occupied my mind – drugs! I had no desire for anything else! As at that time, I could not imagine any life without drugs. I had no time for food or sleep. Everything I did revolve around drugs; cocaine and heroin. I could make the equivalent of three thousand pounds sterling within one hour and squander the same within another hour and then stayed without money for several days. One day, I could live a luxury life spending time in five-star hotels and the very next day, I could be passing the night in the streets like a common pauper. It was a roller coaster kind of life. Nobody except drug addicts wanted me as their friend. In fact, I had no friends. Drug addicts came to me because they liked and wanted what I had and not because they liked me. Besides, I was giving them drugs for free.

'Decent' drug dealers came to me because they knew that I had a reputation for moving out drugs faster than so many others and because I was using the drugs myself, would never adulterate it before giving it out. This attracted more customers to me too. I could sell only a little quantity of what they gave me and pay the owner of the merchandise for the whole quantity of drugs I got from them and end up consuming the remaining drugs myself, and anyone around me was guaranteed free highs.

I shunned every good advice! Whoever attempted to advise me to give up the habit became an instant enemy. This I now realise was as a result of pride. At the time I genuinely thought that I knew better than those who tried to advise me. I was proud but didn't realise it then. I was lost in my pride. Nobody could advise me on what to do or how to live my life. It all seemed right then, but I have now seen the consequence first-hand. This is the same way most people are lost in their pride without realising it. And this includes men of God – Apostles, Pastors, Evangelists, Teachers, and Prophets etc.

Jesus said,

> "I am the vine, and you are the branches. He who abides in Me and I in him, bears much fruit, for without Me you can do nothing" (John15:5).

Pride is one of the greatest enemies of man! Most bad decisions are borne out of pride. Hence, I will devote a more significant part of my write-up on this number one enemy.

Overweening pride, arrogance, haughtiness: these have been the stuff of tragedy. Vanity, fussiness, delicacy: the stuff of comedy. These are all forms of self-delusion, and paper-thin masks over rotting features. Pride and vanity refuse the truth about who we are and substitute illusions for reality. While vanity is mostly concerned with appearance, pride is based in a real desire to be God, at least in one's circle.

The first requirement of pride is spiritual blindness. Such was my situation when I refused good counsel.

There is no doubt that the Spirit of Pride is one of the greatest weapons in the devil's arsenal which he uses to inflict scars on Christians. The devil knows that our God hates pride and that because of pride, he was thrown out of heaven and is destined to live in hell, so he uses that tool to pull so many to himself and cause them to miss heaven with Jesus. Satan did not commit adultery or fornication. He did not steal anything, but he still lost his position due to pride. He was a great singer, providing for God the only thing He loves, worship, yet due to pride, he lost his place.

> *"There are six things the Lord hates, seven that are detestable to Him: haughty eyes, a lying tongue, hands that shed innocent blood, a heart that devices wicked schemes, feet that are quick to rush into evil, a false witness who pours out lies and a person who stirs up conflict in the community" (Proverbs 6:16-19).*

The word haughty is defined by Merriam-Webster as "blatantly and disdainfully proud." The word is always used in the Bible in the evil sense of "arrogant, disdainful and setting oneself above others", it is often set in contrast to being humble.

In Proverbs 21:4, the word 'haughty' is used along with a proud heart. To have haughty eyes is to have an arrogant demeanour; it is an overall attitude of one's heart that causes one to scorn or "look down on" others. The haughty person sets himself above others and ultimately above God. When we are haughty we become the centre of our universe; everything revolves around us. There is little, if any, concern for what others think and no consideration for the will of God. Pride, haughtiness, is the trunk of the tree from which all our sins sprout. When we are at the centre of our world, then nothing that we want is unlawful to us. As my General Overseer will say, people should be careful of how they address those under them because they too are human beings crafted in the image of God and His Son, Jesus died for them too.

God is resistant to haughtiness. Over and over in Scripture, we read that God brings down the haughty and the proud.

> "For You will save the humble people but will bring down haughty looks" (Proverbs 18:27).

> "The lofty looks of man shall be humbled, the haughtiness of men shall be bowed down, and the Lord alone shall be exalted in that day" (Isaiah 2:11).

"People shall be brought down, each man shall be humbled, and the eyes of the lofty shall be humbled. But the Lord of hosts shall be exalted in judgement, and God who is holy shall be hallowed in righteousness" (Isaiah 5:15).

"And they were haughty and committed abomination before Me. Therefore I took them away as I saw fit" (Ezekiel 16:50).

Haughtiness precedes destruction.

"Pride goes before destruction, and a haughty spirit before a fall" (Proverbs 16:18).

"Before destruction the heart of a man is haughty, and before honour is humility" (Proverbs 18:12)

The New Testament is clear on the dangers of arrogance, repeatedly warning against it.

Both James and Peter warned that God actively opposes the proud.

"But He gives more grace. Therefore, He says, "God resists the proud but gives grace to the humble" (James 4:6).

"Being filled with all unrighteousness, fornication, wickedness, covetousness, maliciousness, full of envy, murder, debate, deceit, malignity, whisperers, backbiters,

haters of God, despiteful, proud, boasters, inventors of evil things, disobedient to parents, without understanding, covenant breakers, without natural affection, implacable, unmerciful; Who knowing the judgement of God, that they which commit such things are worthy of death, not only do the same, but have pleasure in them that do them" (Romans 1:29-32).

This means that although one may not do it directly. Siding with, supporting or covering those who do, makes them both equally guilty of the offence.

In the layman's parlance, pride goes before a fall. Someone rightly defined Pride as the "beginning of the end."

A divorced Single Mother wrote this as advice to other people so they can avoid the same error she made:

"I am writing to you in order to make someone understand that it is okay to appreciate our partners despite his or her flaws."

"I am 32 years of age. My ex-husband and I dated for six years. We were best friends. I waited until he completed college and started work. My family and his family then met. We got married and had a son (7 years old now). My husband was short-tempered at times, but our problems started when I wanted to make him feel he could not control me. Every time we argued, I would pack my bags, go to my family and explain. My sisters would phone my husband and shout at him. If he were controlling me, I would always dare him that if he wished, he could divorce me. I never wanted divorce though. I just had pride, and I never wanted to look like a loose woman in his eyes. One day I pushed him so hard that for the first time he beat me and locked me outside. I went to my family, my family took him to the Police and alleged that I was abused continuously. But to be honest, I used to abuse my husband emotionally. He was arrested and detained. I was asked by his family to withdraw the case. I felt that what I was doing was wrong. My husband was never a violent man. He did what he did because I pushed him to the wall of which he openly knelt down and apologised. I withdrew the charge but refused to reconcile with him, but instead remained with my family."

"After three months, I received a call that he was in the hospital. My family told me that I should not go there because it would look like I was begging him and my sisters believed he was feigning the illness. All this time, people felt sorry for me like I was the one being abused. He spent a week in the hospital. After he came out, I just received a divorce summons. I wanted to say no to divorce, but because I felt this pride, I wanted him to change his mind and beg me. I called him and said he would get the divorce because staying with him was like living in hell. When we went to court, I wanted to make him pay, so I told the court that I needed his properties to be shared. To my surprise, he openly told the court that whatever he and I acquired together should be given to me, all he wanted was a divorce. We divorced in July 2009. Now my husband is married, while I am here wasted. My family members are gossiping about me. I depend on what ex-husband gives to my son for survival. I know I wasted my marriage. I am here telling all wives that they should be careful how they get advice. Don't be cheated, don't entertain family interference in your marriage my dear reader. Even my young sisters are much more respected than me. Those who encouraged me to get divorced are always teasing me and bad mouthing me. Please, ladies, be vigilant in your marriage. Thought it wise to share my story to save your marriage. There is practically no benefit in being proud for no reason."

Sometimes, it is not the man's fault at all. It is your pride, and the people you allow to advise you. So be wise and vigilant in your marriage."

Proverbs 13:20 says that,

> *"He who moves with the wise shall be wise, but the companion of fools shall be destroyed."*

> *"Likewise you younger people, submit yourselves to your elders. Yes, all of you be submissive to one another and be clothed with humility, for God resists the proud but gives grace to the humble. Therefore humble yourselves under the mighty hand of God, that He may exalt you in due time"* (1 Peter 5:5-6).

Humility is the quality of having a modest or low view of one's importance.

Jesus is the Lion of the tribe of Judah, yet He is the Lamb of God. A true disciple of Jesus Christ must copy Him in everything. Only that way will people call him a Christian; Christlike.

In the words of A. W. Tozer, "We cannot afford to set aside Christian standards and values just to sustain the interest of people who want to go to hell and still belong to the church.

Men and women who understand "GRACE" remain humble, kind, calm and respectful to the core. Grace knows that what you have, what you are today, who you are now, and what you have achieved so far, are things you do not merit at all.

James 4:6 says,

> *"And He gives grace generously. As the Scriptures say, "God opposes the proud but gives grace to the humble." So humble yourselves before God. Resist the devil, and he will flee from you.""*

> *"He crowns the humble with victory"* (Psalm 149:4).

A humble man will always have victories because God will never stop blessing him. It does not matter how anyone tries to camouflage pride, God hates it and the proud will always lose in the end.

Just like I was so proud during the wilderness period of my life, I sincerely thought I had it all made and did not need God. Instead of seeking God, I was going to herbalists and cultists. In my quest for a solution to my addiction problem, I became a disciple of a famous 'man of God' somewhere in Eastern Nigeria at the time. This man was well revered by his followers as a 'god.' I spent a couple of years with him in the false hopes that my problems would be solved. I would travel all the way from India to Nigeria to worship in this 'church' almost every month, but the expected deliverance did not happen until I met the Lord Jesus in prison.

Any life that excludes God Almighty is pride, and that is foolishness. Anyone who claims to have God yet lives proudly is a liar and must be serving his father, Satan the devil, who is the father of all lies (John 8:44).

No wonder the bible says in Proverbs 10:27 that,

> *"The fear of the Lord prolongs days: but the years of the wicked shall be shortened".*

Malachi 4:1-3 says,

> *"For behold, the day is coming, burning like an oven, and all the proud, yes, all who do wickedly will be stubble. And the day which is coming shall burn them up, says the Lord of hosts. That will leave them neither root nor branch. But you who fear My name, The Sun of Righteousness shall arise with healing in His wings, and you shall go out and grow fat like stall-fed calves. You shall trample the wicked, for they shall be ashes under the soles of your feet. On the day that I do this, says the Lord."*

Who is he who wants to live a long life? Let him have the fear of the Lord and cease from being proud.

People whose lives are ruled by the spirit of pride will invariably be ruined by that same spirit unless they check themselves. Some have gotten so full of themselves that they can even talk to others anyhow, as though they have become God to be worshipped by all. My advice to anyone who thinks they have arrived is this: Please treat the people you meet on your way up with humility, respect and dignity because those are the same people you must meet on your way down.

Always respect everyone no matter the position they occupy in life.

One day the Minister of Agriculture in a certain land went to see how their Beekeeping program was going on. When he reached the gate, the security in charge told him that it was already late and nobody was allowed to go in there after a certain hour.

The Minister got very angry and fumed at the gateman, shouting at him, "Do you know who I am?" (typical of those who are power drunk), while pulling out his ID card from his pocket and hurriedly pushed his way in, leaving the security man puzzled and agape at such pomposity from a boss. (Reminds me of Haman and Mordechai). After a few minutes, the Minister was heard crying and shouting: "Gateman, gateman, help me, the bees are killing me, help me please…"

The gateman simply replied, "Sir, maybe they do not know who you are, just show them your ID card!"

Anyone who lacks the spirit of humility must exhibit the spirit of pride because it is evident that nature does not permit a vacuum.

None of us is immune to pride, and according to Apostle Paul, we are not ignorant of the devices of the devil. The Bible tells us of good people who were brought down in one way or another by pride.

God is the only employer who gives an employee the sack and still allows him to be working even though he has been sacked from his position. Long after the Spirit of God had departed from Saul, God still left him to reign as king in Israel.

1 Samuel 16:14 says,

> *"But the Spirit of the Lord departed from Saul, and a distressing spirit from the Lord troubled him."*

It is worthy of note that even though the Spirit of the Lord had departed from Saul, he still occupied the position of a king. Most servants of God are still being called Men of God even after the Spirit of the Lord had long departed.

Brethren, there is a difference between the Spirit of the Lord and a distressing spirit from the Lord.

Which one do you prefer? Acts 5:32 says, "And we are His witnesses to these things, and so also is the

Holy Spirit whom God has given to those who obey Him."

God gives the Holy Spirit, His Spirit only to those who obey Him and the obedience must be total.

The same thing happened to Samson. Judges 16:20 says,

> *"Then she called Samson; the Philistines are upon you. He awoke from his sleep and thought, I'll go out as before and shake myself free. But he did not know that the Lord had left him."*

I once overheard a leader of a big Church say that one day as he was praying to the Lord, he heard the Holy Spirit whisper to him that God was silent to his prayers because the last time he was told to apologise to a member of his congregation whom he had spoken to in a very unkind and hurtful manner, he did not heed to the instruction, neither did he repent. In his mind, he did not see any reason why he should not treat people under him or talk to them however he chose to. He did not see why he should apologise to a "small man", forgetting that every man is made in God's image and that Jesus Christ died for all. The Lord had long left him even though he was still the "leader" who knew how to preach and quote scriptures. His gifts were still very intact, just as the

Bible states in Romans 11:29 (AMPC), "For God's gifts and His call are irrevocable; He never withdraws them when once they are given, and He does not change His mind about those to whom He gives His grace or to whom He sends His call." The Lord of the gifts had departed from him. He still had the gifts but didn't have the God of the gifts on his side. He was not going to have anything with him until he had obeyed and apologised to the "small man." This is the consequence of pride. It alienates one from his Maker. God sacks one from His employment and still leaves him to work. Isn't God humorous?

As Christians, we should learn not to look down on people because everybody can rise. If humans can make a delicious soup from bitter leaf, God can make a delicious life from a bitter experience. He is Master in getting out a message out of a mess.

Another Pastor friend wrote this following her repentance after the Holy Spirit dealt with her for being so proud while trying to cover it with the so much abused slogans of "I am boasting in the Lord" and "Touch not my anointed." She told me how the Lord dealt with her for using the pulpit to denigrate the same people the Lord had called him to restore from the place the devil had battered them.

She said, "As a Pastor, never use the PULPIT as a battlefield to fight your members who offend you. You know you are not preaching even though you quoted a scripture.

They know you are lashing them, shooting them bullets from the pulpit, and they cannot defend themselves. They listen to your "preaching" with heaviness of heart, and I think that is petty. That is quenching the Spirit."

Remember you do not have the power to draw any man to God. Jesus said to Peter, "If you love Me, FEED MY SHEEP." Do not KILL MY SHEEP (interpretation mine).

When next you feel offended by a member, RESIST fighting them from the PULPIT. Be bold enough to call them to order privately; they will respect you more.

The PULPIT is not for the preaching of offence but for dispensing the knowledge of the person of Jesus. Don't waste that 45 minutes. It counts to God.

The PULPIT is a place to stand and 'pull' people out from the 'pit' and not where you stand and push them further into the pit from where Jesus wants to pull them out. That is where it is called PULPIT.

As a matter of fact, anyone who is proud and boastful is not wise, and such a person will always certainly show partiality in judgement especially when it has to do with those people who sing his praise. Such people find it very difficult to differentiate loyalists from sycophants. Even that leaves a scar at the end of the day.

I learnt from someone that the very church which the world likes best is sure to be the church which God hates most. Can we be called God's ambassadors if we are not representing Him precisely in the terms He has dictated just because we need to compromise or bend the truth? Would we translate the Bible according to our terms and comforts without hoping to pay for it at last?

If an ambassador of a country fails to represent his President the way he is expected to do, the President will recall him unceremoniously. Therefore, as ambassadors of Christ, we should strive to represent our Government exactly the way the Master has directed, so we are not called back home unceremoniously.

2 Timothy 3:1-9 (MSG) says,

> "Don't be naïve. There are difficult times ahead. As the end approaches, people are going to be self-absorbed, money-hungry, self-promoting, stuck-up, profane, contemptuous of parents, crude, coarse, dog-eat-dog,

unbending, slanderers, impulsively wild, savage, cynical, treacherous, ruthless, bloated windbags, addicted to lust, and allergic to God. They will make a show of religion, but behind the scenes they are animals. Stay clear of these people. These are the kind of people who smooth-talk themselves into the homes of unstable and needy women who, depressed by their sinfulness, take up with every new religious fad that calls itself "truth." They get exploited every time and never really learn. These men are like those old Egyptian frauds Jannes and Jambres, who challenged Moses. They were rejects from the faith, twisted in their thinking, defying truth itself. But nothing will come of these latest impostors. Everyone will see through them, just as people saw through that Egyptian hoax."

Brethren, it is only a matter of time, and everything that is hidden shall be exposed.

Serving God acceptably does not begin with service, but it begins with being.

It does not take anything for a big work to be discarded by God. Some get angry even on the pulpit and use their position to abuse people. If once a Christian does not always mean a Christian, then being a Man of God does not mean one will always be a man of God. One anger will cancel out many years of great wisdom.

James 4:4-7 (ESV) says clearly,

> *"You adulterous people! Do you not know that friendship with the world is enmity with God? Therefore, whoever wishes to be a friend of the world makes himself an enemy of God. Or do you suppose it is no purpose that the scripture says, "He yearns jealously over the spirit that He has made to dwell in us"? But He gives more grace. Therefore, it says, God opposes the proud but gives grace to the humble. Submit yourselves therefore to God. Resist the devil, and he will flee from you."*

The Message Translation puts it this way,

> *"You are cheating on God. If all you want is your own way, flirting with the world every chance you get, you end up enemies of God and His way. And do you suppose God does not care? The proverb has it that "He a fiercely jealous lover." And what He gives in love is far better than anything else you'll find. It is common knowledge that God goes against the willful proud; God gives grace to the willing humble." So let God work His will in you. Yell a loud no to the Devil and watch him scamper. Say a quiet yes to God, and He'll be there in no time."*

I love the subtitle in Proverbs 24:23-25: "Further Sayings Of The Wise."

> *"These things also belong to the wise: It is not good to show partiality in judgement. He who says to the wicked, "You are righteous," him the people will curse; nations will abhor him. But those who rebuke the wicked will have delight, and a good blessing will come upon them."*

I was at the first meeting of several Nigerian Pastors which took place at New Wine Church in London while we were planning to celebrate Nigeria's fiftieth year of independence which subsequently took place at Excel, London. At the meeting, I recall saying to the "Generals" in attendance when I had the privilege to speak, that even though I was the least of all the pastors there present, that in my little walk with the Lord then, I had already observed that it is much easier to approach God than to approach some Nigerian men/women of God. Those present laughed, but at the end of that meeting, some of the pastors walked up to say to me that I did hit the nail on the head. In other words, I said it exactly how it is. It is important to remember that we are men of God and not God of men.

God so abhors haughtiness that He expressly forewarned in Micah 2 how the end of the proud would be.

Judgement against wealthy oppressors (NLT).

> "What sorrow awaits you who lie awake at night, thinking up evil plans. You rise at dawn and hurry to carry them out, simply because you have the power to do so. When you want a piece of land, you find, you find a way to seize it. When you want someone's house, you take it by fraud and violence. You cheat a man of his property, stealing his family's inheritance." But this is what the Lord says: "I will reward your evil with evil; You won't be able to pull your neck out of the noose. You will no longer walk around PROUDLY, for it will be a TERRIBLE time. In that day your enemies will make fun of you by singing this song of despair about you: We are finished, completely ruined! God has confiscated our land, taking it from us. He has given our fields to those who betrayed us. Others will set your boundaries then, and the Lord's people will have no say in how the land is divided."

What an end that will be, all because of PRIDE! No wonder, King Solomon himself said in Proverbs 29:23,

> "Pride ends in humiliation, while humility brings honor" (NLT)

"Pride brings a person low, but the lowly in spirit gain honor" (NIV).

"A man's pride and sense of self-importance will bring him down, but he who has a humble spirit will obtain honor" (AMP).

"A man's pride will bring him low, but the humble in spirit will RETAIN honor" (NKJV).

This means that honor can be lost as a result of pride. It is exactly what Jesus says in Matthew 7:21-22,

"Not everyone who calls out to Me, Lord! Lord! Will enter the kingdom of Heaven. Only those who do the will of My Father in heaven will enter. On Judgement Day, many will say to Me, Lord! Lord! We prophesied in Your name and cast out demons in Your name and performed many miracles in your name."

In 1 Corinthians 5:6-8, Apostles Paul wrote thus:

"Your glorying is not good. Do you not know that a little leaven leavens the whole lump? Therefore purge out the old leaven, that you may be a new lump since you truly are unleavened. For indeed Christ, our Passover was sacrificed for us. Therefore let us keep the feast, not with old leaven, nor with the leaven of malice and wickedness, but with the unleavened bread of sincerity and truth."

NOT WITHOUT A SCAR

Sometimes, even as Christians, we deceive ourselves by claiming that we are boasting in the Lord when in fact we are boastful in ourselves. These things leave scars that only a full turnaround from our old boastful ways can wipe away.

Anything we do on earth that does not land us in heaven is waste. What is the point of going to church and ending up in hell with those who did not know Christ at all?

In Antioch, the followers of Christ were called Christians, which means "little Christs." The only thing their life reminded the people of Antioch was Christ. Hence they gave them the title, Christians.

What is the point of receiving Christ and ending in hellfire? What shall it profit a man if he spends his whole life in church and still ends in hell?

Pride is one major trap the devil uses to pull Christians into hell.

Everyone who wants to look like Christ should look at Christ. You resemble what you look like.

2 Corinthians 3:18 says,

> "But we all, with open face beholding as in a glass the glory of the Lord, are changed into the same image from glory to glory, even as by the Spirit of the Lord."

A proud person will never accept that they have gotten anything wrong, not even when they sin against God. Pride is a very dangerous evil. Many people may preach great messages, perform great miracles and still miss heaven.

2 Corinthians 7:10-14 captures it succinctly,

> *"For the kind of sorrow God wants us to experience leads us away from sin and results in salvation. There's no regret for that kind of sorrow. But worldly sorrow, which lacks repentance, results in spiritual death. Just see what this godly sorrow produced in you! Such earnestness, such concern to clear yourselves, such indignation, such alarm, such longing to see Me, such zeal, and such a readiness to punish wrong. You showed that you had done everything necessary to make things right. My purpose then was not to write about who did the wrong or who was wronged. I wrote to you so that in the sight of God you could see for yourselves how loyal you are to us. We have been greatly encouraged by this. In addition to our encouragement, we were especially delighted to see how happy Titus was about the way all of you welcomed him and set his mind at ease. I had told him how proud I was of you, and you did not disappoint me. I have always told you the truth, and now my boasting to Titus has also proved true!"* (NLT).

A God-given command on the inside of each person is to become more and multiply. He said I would make you into a great nation, and I will bless you. I will make your name great, and you will be a blessing and all people on earth will be blessed through you (Genesis 12-2-3).

In Matthew 4:19, Jesus said to Peter and his brother, Andrew,

> *"Follow Me, I will make you fishers of men."*

Isaiah 64:8 says,

> *"But now O' Lord, You are our Father; we are the clay, and You our Potter; and we all are the work of Your hand."*

In Romans 9:20-21, Paul writes,

> *"But indeed, O man, who are you to reply against God? Will the thing formed say to Him who formed it, "Why have you made me like this?" Does not the potter have power over the clay; from the same lump to make one vessel for honour and another for dishonour?"*

Isaiah records in his book,

> *"Surely you have things turned around! Shall the Potter be esteemed as the clay; For shall the thing formed say of him who formed it, "He did not make me"? Or shall the thing formed say*

of him who formed it, "He has no understanding"? (Isaiah 29:16).

John 3:27 records that

"Unless heaven releases, NO man can receive."

1 Corinthians 4:7 says,

"What is it you have that you did not receive, and if you received it, how come you behave as if you did not receive it?"

Let me tell this story I heard from a friend of mine which he used to describe the world and its people.

What a world!

A 30-year-old son decided to admit his father into an Old People's Home as desired by his wife. He brought the father in a car to an Old Peoples' Home run by a Catholic Priest.

Then appeared this elderly priest, who came out to have a long chat with the old man. The son wondered and asked the priest whether he knew his father before since they were talking as though they knew each other. The priest replied, yes, and continued, "He came here 30 years back and took with him a very sick orphan boy whom everyone else had rejected for adoption. This man gave that boy home and saved his life. He told us this little boy deserves better and I will dedicate my life to make him the wealthiest young man when he turns 25."

The priest continued, "I do not know how long you have known him but I can tell you he is a good man and I am glad to inform you that you were the sick boy." On hearing this, the boy fell to his knees and begged the old man for forgiveness. The old man looked at him with a smile and said, "Son, I have forgiven you. You threw me out of my own home because of your wife. Take the house but know that I have removed you from my documents as the sole heir of my empire. I have willed all my properties to this orphanage where I now belong.

What is that thing that has taken the place of compassion towards other people from you? Is there anything you have now that is worthy of making you lose the place Jesus has prepared for you? How do you treat your fellow human beings? Like animals for whom Jesus' blood wasn't shed on the Cross? The young man lost an empire because of his attachment to a house he did not even build. We are like that orphan, rejected by all until God's grace located us and gave us a chance to live. How are we showing Him our appreciation? Our love for God is measured by our love for our neighbour. We are our brother's keeper, unlike Cain who said he was not. At the end of time, it is only our love for our neighbour that shows that we are God's ambassadors. In John 13:34-35, Jesus says, "A new commandment I give to you, that you love one another as I have loved you, that you also love one another. By this, all will know that you are My disciples if you have love for one another."

At the height of your success don't forget where you are coming from. If not, you will miss your destination and lose your Crown.

Chapter Five
BIBLICAL EXAMPLES

The Bible has a list of names of those who walked with God but the hasty or wrong decisions they made left an everlasting scar on them. We will look into a few of those names and see what each of them did and the mark it left.

ADAM AND EVE

In Genesis 1:27, we read,

> *"So God created man in His own image; in the image of God He created him; male and female He created them."*

So the man was already like God Himself. However, man was fooled by the subtlety of the serpent who now made man believe that by disobeying God, he would be like God. In Matthew 4 and Luke 4, the devil tried the same trick with Jesus Christ the only begotten Son of God the Father, by suggesting to Him that if He was the Son of God etc. You do not need anyone to tell you who you are. Jesus knew who He was on the earth and wouldn't be deceived by the devil. No not even for a moment. Adam and Eve, on the contrary, allowed themselves to be deceived and they lost their place in the Garden of Eden. Because of this disobedience, the blessing they received from God in Genesis 1:28, was replaced with a curse in Genesis 3:16-19. Every act of disobedience to God attracts a punishment and ultimately leaves a scar. The first murder took place in this family. These are some of the ways sin opens doors to the devil. Adam had the privilege of naming everything that God created. He was the first living being that God formed, and He made Him look like God Himself. He enjoyed the privilege of being visited by God Himself on a daily basis.

One would have thought that nothing else would have mattered to Him in life other than God's presence. He had everything well laid out for him in the Garden. Toiling was not part of the plan at all. All he had to do was to nurture the Garden and tend it. However, as a consequence of his momentary mistake, he did not only lose the privilege of being visited by God, he also lost his privileged place in the garden. Toiling was also introduced into his life. That was not God's original plan for him and Eve.

Many things may look pleasant to the eyes but may not necessarily leave a good taste in the mouth. Often, the choice we make regarding anything leaves a lasting consequence. This is why we need to reflect before we do anything.

Anyone who allows himself to be used as a door for the devil to enter into any place will also suffer the punishment the Lord will give to the devil. There are consequences for whatever choices we make in life. The serpent was used as a gateway for the devil to enter into the Garden of Eden and ended up receiving an everlasting curse from God.

Genesis 3:14-15 reads,

> *"Then the Lord said to the serpent, because you have done this, you are cursed more than all animals, domestic and wild. You will crawl on your belly, grovelling in the dust as long as you live. And I will cause hostility between you and the woman, and between your offspring and her offspring. He will strike your head, and you will strike his heel."*

As my Pastor would say, "If you eat what you shouldn't be eating, you will be hit with the heat you shouldn't be experiencing." That is the consequence. Being hit with the heat is the price you pay. It is the cost of your action. It is the scar you will be left with after the scourge.

UZZIAH (2 Chronicles 26:1-23)

"Now all the people of Judah took Uzziah, who was sixteen years old, and made him king instead of his father, Amaziah. He built Elath and restored it to Judah after the king rested with his fathers. Uzziah was sixteen years old when he became king, and he reigned fifty-two years in Jerusalem. His mother's name was Jecholiah of Jerusalem. And he did what was right in the sight of the Lord, according to all that his father Amaziah had done. He sought God in the days of Zechariah, who had understanding in the visions of God; as long as he sought the Lord, God made him prosper. Now he went out and made war against the Philistines, and broke down the wall of Gath, the wall of Jabneh, and the wall of Ashdod; and he built cities around Ashdod and among the Philistines. God helped him against the Philistines, against the Arabians who lived in Gur Baal, and against Meunites. Also, the Ammonites brought tribute to Uzziah. His fame spread as far as the entrance of Egypt, for he became exceedingly strong. And Uzziah built towers in Jerusalem at the Corner Gate, at the Valley Gate, and at the corner buttress

of the wall: then he fortified them. Also, he built towers in the desert. He dug many wells, for he had so much livestock, both in lowlands and in plains; he also had farmers and vinedressers in the mountains and in Carmel, for he loved the soil. Moreover, Uzziah had an army of fighting men who went out to war by companies, according to the number on their roll as prepared by Jeiel the scribe and Maaseiah, the officer, under the hand of Hananiah, one of the king's captains. The total number of chief officers of the mighty men of valour` was two thousand six hundred. And under their authority was an army of three hundred and seven thousand five hundred, that made war with mighty power, to help the king against the enemy. Then Uzziah prepared for them, for the entire army, shields, spears, helmets, body armour, bows, and slings to cast stones. And he made devices in Jerusalem, invented by skilful men, to be on the towers and the corners, to shoot arrows and large stones. So his fame spread far and wide, for he was marvellously helped till he became strong. But when he was strong, his heart was lifted up, to his destruction, for he transgressed against the Lord his God by entering the temple of the Lord to burn incense on the altar of incense. So Azariah the priest went in after him, and with him were eighty priests of the Lord - valiant men. And they withstood King

Uzziah and said to him, "It is not for you, Uzziah, to burn incense to the Lord, but for the priests, the sons of Aaron, who are consecrated to burn incense. Get out of the sanctuary, for you have trespassed! You shall have no honour from the Lord God." Then Uzziah became furious, and he had a censer in his hand to burn incense. And while he was angry with the priests, leprosy broke out on his forehead, before the priests in the house of the Lord, beside the incense altar. And Azariah the chief priest and all the priests looked at him, and there, on his forehead, he was leprous; so they thrust him out of that place. Indeed, he also hurried to get out, because the Lord had struck him. King Uzziah was a leper until the day of his death. He dwelt in an isolated house because he was a leper; for he was cut off from the house of the Lord. Then Jotham his son was over the king's house, judging the people of the land. Now the rest of the acts of Uzziah, from first to last, the prophet Isaiah the son of Amoz wrote; So Uzziah rested with his fathers in the field of burial which belonged to the kings, for they said, "He is a leper." Then Jotham his son reigned in his place."

A closer look at verses 15-16 of the above scripture will show us that Uzziah's heart was lifted up only after he became influential in his ministry. Often, you see Christians who show great humility while they are yet climbing the ladder; they will do all that is necessary to get people to support them in their endeavours but no sooner than they feel that they "have arrived", than the spirit of pride takes them over. The line between humility and pride is so thin that some people do not even realise when they have crossed over from humility to pride, and that is exactly all that the devil wants to happen so that he will not go to hell unaccompanied.

Another thing is that the moment his heart was lifted in pride, he no longer was able to remain in his office of calling but moved into another's office. When you see anyone leaving their assignment to encroach into another's simply because he or she feels an air of importance, you have just seen someone manifesting the spirit of arrogance.

God has always frowned at pride, and we can see that Uzziah and Lucifer are not isolated cases. The same thing happened to Jeshurun.

JESHURUN (Deuteronomy 32:10-29)

> *"In a desert land, He found him, in a barren and howling waste. He shielded him and cared for him; He guided him as the apple of His eye, like an eagle that stirs up the nest and hovers over its young, that spreads its wings to catch*

them and carries them aloft. The Lord alone led him. He made him ride on the heights of the land and fed him with the fruit of the fields. He nourished him with honey from the rock, and with oil from the flinty crag, with curds and milk from herd and flock and with fattened lambs and goats, with choice rams of Bashan and the finest kernels of wheat. You drank the foaming blood of the grape. Jeshurun grew fat and kicked; filled with food, they became heavy and sleek. They abandoned the God who made them and rejected the Rock their Saviour. They made Him jealous with their foreign gods and angered Him with their detestable idols. They sacrificed to false gods, which are not God — gods they had not known, gods that recently appeared, gods your ancestors did not fear. You deserted the Rock, who fathered you; you forgot the God who gave you birth. The Lord saw this and rejected them because He was angered by His sons and daughters. I will hide My face from them, "He said, and see what their end will be; for they are a perverse generation, children who are unfaithful." They made Me jealous by what is no god and angered Me with their worthless idols. I will make them envious by those who are not people; I will make them angry by a nation that has no understanding. For a fire will be kindled by My wrath, one that burns down to the realm of the dead below. I will devour the earth and its harvests and set afire foundations of the mountains. I will heap calamities on them and spend My arrows against them. I will send wasting famine against them, consuming pestilence and deadly plague; I will send against them the fangs of wild beasts, the venom of vipers that glide in the dust. In the street, the sword will make them childless; in their homes, terror will reign. The young men and young women will perish, the infants and those with grey hair. I said I will scatter them and erase their name from human memory, but I dreaded the taunt of the enemy, lest the adversary misunderstand and say, "Our hand has triumphed; the Lord has not done all this." They are a nation without sense; there is no discernment in them. If only they were wise and would understand this and discern what their end will be"

In other words, if only they could see where the spirit of pride was to drive them to.

MEPHIBOSHETH

After David had restored all that Saul and Jonathan had to Mephibosheth, and commanded Ziba and his sons to become Mephibosheth's servants, Mephibosheth lost everything due to pride mixed with greed.

"Then the king summoned Ziba, Saul's steward, and said to him, "I have given your master's grandson everything that belonged to Saul and his family. You and your sons and your servants are to farm the land for him and bring in the crops, so that your master's grandson may be provided for. And Mephibosheth, grandson of your master, will always eat at my table." (Now Ziba had fifteen sons and twenty servants.) Then Ziba said to the king, "Your servant will do whatever my lord the king commands his servant to do. "So Mephibosheth ate at David's table like one of the king's sons. Mephibosheth had a young son named Mika, and all the members of Ziba's household were servants of Mephibosheth. And Mephibosheth lived in Jerusalem because he always ate at the king's table; he was lame in both feet" (2 Samuel 9:9-13).

When we talk of speedy restoration, Miphiboseth's case is a good example. This was a man who had lost his place and lost every form of dignity. He was living in Lo Debar but was suddenly brought to eat at the king's table. Unfortunately, he lost everything in one day.

Mephibosheth loses all (2 Samuel 16:3-4).

"The king then asked, "Where is your master's grandson?" Ziba said to him, "He is staying

> *in Jerusalem, because he thinks, "Today the*
> *Israelites will restore to me my grandfather's*
> *kingdom." Then the king said to Ziba, "All*
> *that belongs to Mephibosheth is now yours."*
> *"I humbly bow," Ziba said. "May I find favour*
> *in your eyes, my lord the king."*

After experiencing the goodness of God in any area of their lives, some Christians start behaving as though it was by their power that those things happened. In fact, some after enjoying the services of other people when they were in need, will subsequently turn around and boast that their connection, wisdom and intelligence gave them the breakthrough, forgetting that it is not of him that wills nor of him that runs, but of God that shows mercy.

MOSES

Moses was described as the meekest man, an example of humility in Numbers 12:3. He had a great place in God's plan for the redemption of the Israelites from their bondage in Egypt. He had the privilege of speaking with God on Mount Sinai (Exodus 3). God told him that He had made him as god unto Pharaoh and that Aaron his brother shall be his prophet. What a privilege! He spoke with God on behalf of the

Israelites. He was meant to take them to the Promised Land even by the Red Sea (Exodus 6).

He was so zealous for the things of God that he even became a murderer (Exodus 2:12). God performed some great miracles through him that even his rod became a serpent (Exodus 7:10). He stretched out his hand over the Red Sea, and the Lord caused the sea to go back by a strong east wind and made the sea become a dry land for the children of Israel to cross to the Promised Land (Exodus 14:21). In Exodus 17:1-7, Moses received the express instruction from God to strike the rock with his rod and see water come out of it. He obeyed God and saw the result. His position was so much unique that one would have believed that nothing was ever going to stop him from getting to the Promised Land. One single act of disobedience was able to stop him and bring his ministry to a premature end. As a result of one singular act of disobedience, the Lord said to him in Numbers 27:14,

> "For in the Wilderness of Zin, during the strife of the congregation, you rebelled against My command to hallow Me at the waters before their eyes. These are the waters of Meribah, Kadesh in the Wilderness of Zin."

Matthew 24:13 says that it is only he who endures until the end that will be saved. It is not how one starts, but how one ends that is important. There is a need to watch and pray.

Ezekiel 18:24 and Ezekiel 33:18 say that If a righteous person turns from their righteousness and commits sin and does the same detestable things the wicked person does, will they live? None of the righteous things that person has done will be remembered. They will die.

Numbers 20:7-13,

> *"Then the Lord spoke to Moses, saying, "Take the rod, you and your brother Aaron gather the congregation together. Speak to the rock before their eyes, and it will yield its water; thus you shall bring water for them out of the rock, and give drink to the congregation and their animals. So Moses took the rod from before the Lord as He commanded him. And Moses and Aaron gathered the assembly together before the rock, and he said to them, "Hear now you rebels! Must we bring water for you out of this rock?" Then Moses lifted up his hand and struck the rock twice with his rod; and water came out abundantly, and the congregation and their animals drank. Then the Lord spoke to Moses and Aaron, "Because you did not believe Me, to hallow Me in the eyes of the children of Israel, therefore you shall not bring this assembly into the land which I have given*

them. This was the water of Meribah because the children of Israel contended with the Lord, and He was hallowed among them."

Further down in verse 24, the Lord said,

"Aaron shall be gathered to His people, for he shall not enter the land which I have given to the children of Israel because you rebelled against My word at the water of Meribah."

The fact that Moses enjoyed such a privileged position with God was not a guarantee that he would get to the Promised Land. Moses had the spirit of obedience inside of him but chose instead not to put it to use. It is apparent that he made his own choice. For instance, when the Lord told Moses that he would not take His people to the Promised Land, Moses said to Him in Numbers 27:16-20,

"Let the Lord, the God of the spirits of all flesh, set a man over the congregation, who may go out before them, who may lead them out and bring them in, that the congregation of the Lord may not be like sheep which have no shepherd." And the Lord said to Moses, "Take Joshua the son of Nun with you, a man in whom is the Spirit, and lay your hand on him, set him before Eleazar the priest and before all the congregation, and inaugurate him in their sight, and you shall give some of YOUR

*authority to him, that all the congregation of
the children of Israel may be obedient."*

Moses did not only enjoy the privilege of seeing God and receiving from Him the Ten Commandments; he did not only enjoy the privilege of being sent to Pharaoh even as a god to him; he did not only get water out from the rocks; he did not only kill an Egyptian while defending his brother an Israelite; yet he never got to the Promised Land. Moses disobeyed a direct command from God. He took the credit for bringing forth water from the rock. He took credit for the miracle rather than attributing it to God.

Jesus is described as the water-giving rock in 1 Corinthians 10:4. The rock that brought out water was to be struck only once, and that had already taken place in Exodus 17:6, just as Christ was crucified once as we read in Hebrews 7:27. God had commanded Moses to speak to the rock in Numbers 20, as a picture of prayer, (speaking to the Rock), instead he angrily struck the rock, in effect, crucifying Christ a second time.

His punishment for disobedience, pride, and the misrepresentation of Christ's sacrifice was that he was barred from entering the Promised Land (Numbers 20:12).

Any believer, especially a Christian leader, who finds themselves in any of these must know that there is an ugly scar already on them, since the Bible states clearly in Ephesians 5:27,

> *"That He might present her (the Church) to Himself a glorious Church, not having spot or wrinkle or any such thing, but that she should be holy and without blemish."*

This means that anyone He will present to Himself shall be without scars.

In Matthew 8:9, the Centurion said to Jesus,

> *"For I also am a man under authority, having soldiers under me. And I say to this one, "Go", and he goes; and to another, "Come," and he comes; and to my servant, "Do this and that, and he does." When Jesus heard it, He marvelled, and said to those who followed, "Assuredly, I say to you, I have not found such great faith, not even in Israel! But the sons of the kingdom will be cast out into outer darkness. There will be weeping and gnashing of teeth."*

It is in hellfire that there will be gnashing of teeth. Where one ends has nothing to do with where they were born or even how they started but how they finished, and this is entirely based on the choices they made here on earth even if they were a powerfully anointed man or woman of God.

Chapter Six
THE UNDOING OF KING SAUL

In Judges 17:6 and 21:25, the Bibles says that in those days there was no king in Israel; everyone did what was right in his own eyes. At that time also, Hannah was being taunted by Peninnah because she had no child. However, by the grace of God she realised that the gap for a prophet needed to be filled, so she made a vow to God in 1 Samuel 1:11, promising to give her son back to God should He give her one in other that God will use the son she received from His hands to resolve the problem. Once she got the desire of her heart met, she also had to fulfil her vow to God. In fact, in 1 Samuel 1:27-28, Hannah said, "For this child I prayed, and the Lord has granted me my petition which I asked of Him. Therefore I also have lent him to the Lord; as long as he lives he shall be lent to the Lord. So they worshipped the Lord there."

Hannah realised the importance of fulfilling vows. The Bible says it is better not to make a vow than to make one and don't redeem same. The Bible calls that foolishness (Ecclesiastes 5:4), and only foolish people say that God does not exist.

When Samuel became old, he made his sons judges over Israel. 1 Samuel 8:3-7, 9, 19-22 says:

> *"However, his sons did not walk in his ways; they turned aside after dishonest gain, took bribes and perverted justice. Then all the elders of Israel gathered together and came to Samuel at Ramah, and said to him, "Look, you are old, and your sons do not walk in your ways. Now make us a king to judge us like all the nations. But the thing displeased Samuel when they said, "Give us a king to judge us." So Samuel prayed to the Lord. And the Lord said to Samuel, "Heed the voice of the people in all that they say to you; for they have not rejected you, but they have rejected Me, that I should not reign over them. Now, therefore, heed their voice. However, you shall solemnly forewarn them, and show them the behaviour of the king who will reign over them." Nevertheless, the people refused to obey the voice of Samuel; and they said , "No, but we will have a king over us, that we also may be like all the nations, and that our king may judge us and go out before us and fight our battles. And Samuel heard all the words of the people, and he repeated them in the hearing of the Lord. So the Lord said to Samuel, "Heed their voice, and make them a*

king." And Samuel said every man go to his city."

It is not often when God is pressured into an answer would one have gotten His perfect will. Even when God told Samuel to grant the peoples request, it didn't mean that God was pleased with their demand, we can see a similar scenario played out in Numbers 22, where God said categorically to Balaam,

> *"You shall not go with them; you shall not curse the people, for they are blessed" (verse 12).*

From verses 20-23, we read,

> *"And God came to Balaam at night and said to him, "If the men come to call you, rise and go with them; but only the word which I speak to you, that you shall do. So Balaam rose in the morning, saddled his donkey, and went with the princes of Moab. Then God's anger was aroused because he went, and the Angel of the Lord took His stand in the way as an adversary against him. And he was riding on his donkey, and his two servants were with him. Now the donkey saw the Angel of the Lord standing in the way with His drawn sword in His hand, and the donkey turned aside out of the way and went into the field. So Balaam struck the donkey to turn her back onto the road."*

God asked Samuel to give the people a king after they had pressured Him, but that was not what He wanted for them. He had His plans which will always be better than men's. He says in Jeremiah 29:11,

> *"For I know the thoughts I have towards you, thoughts of peace and not for evil."*

The Bible talks about God's perfect will for man in Romans 12:2. Therefore, even though God had permitted them to have a king as they asked for, He was going to allow them to suffer the consequences of their ungodly demand. In 1 Samuel 9:15-17, we read,

> *"Now the Lord had told Samuel in his ear the day before Saul came, saying, "Tomorrow about this time I will send you a man from the land of Benjamin, and you shall anoint him commander over My people Israel, that he may save My people from the hand of the Philistines; for I have looked upon My people, because their cry has come to Me." So when Samuel saw Saul, the Lord said to him, "There he is, the man of whom I spoke to you. This one shall reign over my people."*

In 1 Samuel 15:1-3, we read,

> *"Samuel also said to Saul, "The Lord sent me to anoint you king over His people, over Israel. Now, therefore, heed the voice of the words of the Lord. Thus says the Lord of hosts; "I will*

punish Amalek for what he did to Israel, how he ambushed him on the way when he came up from Egypt. Now go and attack Amalek, and utterly destroy all that they have, and do not spare them. But kill both a man and woman, infant and nursing child, ox and sheep, camel and donkey."

Now, these were specific instructions and there is nothing confusing about this.

Let's see how Saul obeyed God's instructions to the letters.

"And Saul attacked the Amalekites, from Havilah all the way to Shur, which is east of Egypt. He also took Agag king of the Amalekites alive and utterly destroyed all the people with the edge of the sword. But Saul and the people spared Agag and the best of the sheep, the oxen, the fatlings, the lambs, and all that was good, and were unwilling to destroy them utterly. But everything despised and worthless, that they utterly destroyed. Now the word of the Lord came to Samuel saying, "I greatly regret that I have set up Saul as king, for he has turned back following Me, and has not performed My commandments." And it grieved Samuel, and he cried out to the Lord all night" (1 Samuel 15:7-11).

Further on in 1 Samuel 15:13-28, we read,

> *"Then Samuel went to Saul, and Saul said to him, "Blessed are you of the Lord! I have performed the commandment of the Lord." But Samuel said, "What then is this bleating of sheep in my ears, and the lowing of the oxen which I hear?" And Saul said, "They have brought them from the Amalekites; for the people spared the best of the sheep and the oxen, to sacrifice to the Lord your God; and the rest we have utterly destroyed. Then Samuel said to Saul, "Be quiet! And I will tell you what the Lord said to me last night." And he said to him, "Speak on." So Samuel said, "When you were little in your own eyes, were you not head of the tribes of Israel? And did not the Lord anoint you king over Israel? "Now the Lord sent you on a mission, and said, "Go, and utterly destroy the sinners, the Amalekites, and fight against them until they are consumed." "Why then did you not obey the voice of the Lord? Why did you swoop down on the spoil, and do evil in the sight of the Lord? And Saul said to Samuel, "But I have obeyed the voice of the Lord and gone on the mission on which the Lord sent me, and brought back Agag king of Amalek; I have utterly destroyed the Amalekites. "But the people took of the plunder, sheep and oxen, the best of the things which should have been utterly destroyed, to sacrifice to the Lord your*

God in Gilgal." So Samuel said: Has the Lord as great delight in burnt offerings and sacrifices, As in obeying the voice of the Lord? Behold, to obey is better than sacrifice, And to heed than the fat of rams. For rebellion is as the sin of witchcraft, And stubbornness is as iniquity and idolatry. Because you have rejected the word of the Lord, He also has rejected you from being king. Then Saul said to Samuel, "I have sinned, for I have transgressed the commandment of the Lord and your words because I feared the people and obeyed their voice.   "Now, therefore, please pardon my sin, and return with me, that I may worship the Lord. But Samuel said to Saul, "I will not return with you, for you have rejected the word of the Lord, and the Lord has rejected you from being king over Israel." And as Samuel turned around to go away, Saul seized the edge of his robe, and it tore. So Samuel said to him, "The Lord has torn the kingdom of Israel from you today, and has given it to a neighbour of yours, who is better than you."

Saul refused to follow instructions to the letter. It does not matter how good your intentions may be; the Lord is displeased with anyone who will not follow Him according to His own pre-set standards.

Half obedience is disobedience to God. It is either you obey Him completely, or you are in disobedience. There are no half measures.

In 1 Samuel 13:14, speaking about Saul, the Lord said:

> *"But now your kingdom MUST end, for the Lord has sought out a man after His own heart. The Lord has already appointed him to be the leader of his people because you have not kept the Lord's command" (NLT).*

It does not matter how good one has been; God expects us to say like Apostle Paul in 2 Timothy 4:7,

> *"I have fought a good fight, I have finished the race, I have kept the faith. Finally, there is laid up for me the crown of righteousness, which the Lord, the righteous Judge, will give to me on that Day, and not to me only but also to all who have loved His appearing."*

Another of Saul's weaknesses is his inability to accept that God could raise someone else as king. He did all he could to destroy David whom God had appointed king to replace him. Saul said to his son Jonathan in 1 Samuel 20:30-33,

> *"You stupid son of a whore! Do you think I don't know that you want him to be king in your place, shaming yourself and your*

mother? As long as that son of Jesse is alive, you will never be king. Now go and get him so I can kill him." "But why should he be put to death?" Jonathan asked his father. "What has he done?" The Saul hurled his spear at Jonathan, intending to kill him. So at last Jonathan realised that his father was really determined to kill David."

King Saul was destined to have a glorious ending but his actions brought a curse. He ended badly even though he was the first King Israel had. He was proud. He was arrogant. He was envious of his subject. He ended badly.

2 Samuel 1:21-27 says,

"O mountains of Gilboa, Let there be no dew nor rain upon you, nor fields of offerings. For the shield of the mighty is cast away there! The shield of Saul, not anointed with oil." From the blood of the slain, from the fat of the mighty, the bow of Jonathan did not turn back, and the sword of Saul did not return empty. Saul and Jonathan were beloved and pleasant in their lives, and in their death, they were not divided; they were swifter than eagles, they were stronger than lions. O daughters of Israel, weep over Saul, who clothed you in scarlet, with luxury; who put ornaments of gold on your apparel. How the mighty have fallen in the midst of the battle! Jonathan was slain in

your high places. I am distressed for you, my brother Jonathan; you have been very pleasant to me; your love to me was wonderful, surpassing the love of women. How the mighty have fallen, and the weapons of war perished!"

In 2 Samuel 7:15, the Lord said that it was He who took away His love from Saul.

My Pastor would say: When the shield of the mighty is cast away, the shame of the mighty becomes evident.

Dear friend, who are you jealous of in ministry? Who are you struggling in your spirit to see live? Who is that person whose guts you find difficult to stand? Saul had more influence and power than David, yet he could not stand the idea that David also had the right to be. Are we not all children of the same Father according to John 1:12? What is going on inside the church these days?

The unholy spirit of dog-eat-dog has crept into the House of God, where people do not care how many people they brush aside in other to get to the top. This is different from the spirit of Eli, a man who was accustomed to hearing God's voice. He was not jealous of the young Samuel when he perceived that God had bypassed him the "Pastor" to speak to Samuel. Rather, the moment he perceived that God was speaking to Samuel, he helped Samuel to understand that it was God Himself that was speaking to him, and he taught him how to answer,

> "Speak Lord, Your servant hears" (1 Samuel 3:9).

In one of his letters to the Galatians, Paul wrote this,

> "O foolish Galatians! Who has bewitched you that you should not obey the truth, before whose eyes Jesus Christ was clearly portrayed among you as crucified? This only I want to learn from you: Did you receive the Spirit by the works of the law, or by hearing of faith? Are you so foolish? Having begun in the Spirit, are you now made perfect by the flesh?" Have you suffered so many things in vain—if indeed it was in vain?" (Galatians 3:1-4).

In the things of God and our walk with him, we are expected to improve and not be static. If we were haters and full of envy before we met Christ, it is not permitted that we should remain in that same state. Abraham believed God, and it was accounted to Him for righteousness (Galatians 3:6). It is only through faith that we believe that God exists and knowing through faith that God exists should us make us know that He is a rewarder. What we put in is what we get out. We are not rewarded according to our wish but according to our deed. Saul lost his position because of a wrong decision he made.

Writing to the Colossians, Paul said,

> "But now you yourselves are to put off all these: anger, wrath, malice, blasphemy, filthy language out of your mouth. Do not lie to one another, since you have put off the old man with his deeds, and have put on the new man who is renewed in knowledge according to the image of Him who created him, where there is neither Greek nor Jew, circumcised nor uncircumcised, barbarian, Scythian, slave nor free, but Christ is all and in all. Therefore, as the elect of God, holy and beloved, put on tender mercies, kindness, humility, meekness, longsuffering; bearing with one another, and forgiving one another, if anyone has a complaint against another, even as Christ forgave you, so you also must do. But above all these things put on love, which is the bond of perfection. And let the peace of God rule in your hearts, to which also you were called in one body; and be thankful" (Colossians 3:8-15).

It is rather unfortunate to say that the Church is not demonstrating that love which should be the identity of a Christian in the words of Jesus Christ himself as recorded in John 13:34-35,

> *"A new commandment I give to you, that you love one another; as I have loved you, that you also love one another. By this, all will know that you are My disciples if you have love for one another."*

The Church is no longer one large family. What is prevalent in churches these days are groupings of people and classes and what have you. The effect is that if we find it difficult to love ourselves genuinely in the church, we will find it even much harder to love the unsaved, and the consequence is that souls that are not regenerated will continue to cause problems in the world.

In the Message translation of Matthew 28:18-20, Jesus said,

> *"Jesus, undeterred, went right ahead and gave His charge: "God authorised and commanded Me to commission you: Go out and train everyone you meet, far and near, in this way of life, marking them by baptism in the threefold name: Father, Son, and Holy Spirit. Then instruct them in the practice of all I have commanded you. I'll be with you as you do this, day after day after day, right up to the end of the age."*

How do we train others in the way of life we cannot even boast to be living ourselves? Besides, that Scripture says He will be with us as we carry out that assignment.

Oh, how I love the part of Paul's writings that is subtitled, "Striving for a Crown."

> "Do you not know that those who run in a race all, but one receives the prize? Run in such a way that you may obtain it. And everyone who competes for the prize is temperate in all things. Now they do it to obtain a perishable crown, but we for an imperishable crown. Therefore, I run thus: not with uncertainty. Thus I fight: not as one who beats the air. But I discipline my body and bring it into subjection, lest, when I have preached to others, I myself should become disqualified" (1 Corinthians 9:24-27).

Chapter Seven

MORE BIBLICAL EXAMPLES

JONAH (Jonah 1:1-4)

"Now the word of the Lord came to Jonah the son of Amittai, saying, "Arise, go to Nineveh, that great city, and cry out against it; for their wickedness has come up before Me." But Jonah arose to flee to Tarshish from the presence of the Lord. He went down to Joppa, and found a ship going to Tarshish; so he paid the fare, and went down into it, to go with them to Tarshish from the presence of the Lord. But the Lord sent out a great wind on the sea, and there was a mighty tempest on the sea so that the ship was about to be broken up."

Jonah was another man who thought that he was holier than everyone else and that it was better he went to his own mission than to go to Nineveh, where the Lord had explicitly sent him. He chose instead to flee to Tarshish, from God's presence. What he didn't realise is that nobody is hidden from His presence.

The Bible says in Isaiah 29:15,

> *"Woe to them that seek to hide their plans from God and carry on wickedness in the dark, thinking that they will not be seen or known."*

This defines a hypocrite as one who attempts to deceive God and man.

> *"Where can I go from Your Spirit? Or where can I flee from Your presence? If I ascend into heaven, You are there; If I make my bed in hell, behold, You are there. If I make my bed in hell, behold You are there. If I take the wings of the morning and dwell in the uttermost parts of the sea, Even there Your hands shall lead me, and Your right hand shall hold me. If I say, "Surely the darkness shall fall on me, Even the night shall be light about me; Indeed, the darkness shall not hide from You, but the night shines as the day; the darkness and the light are both alike to You" (Psalm 139:7-12).*

> *"Nothing in all creation is hidden from God. Everything is naked and exposed before His eyes, and He is the One to whom we are accountable" (Hebrews 4:13, NLT).*

There is a song titled "Silent Judge" by one Tope Alabi. The lyrics go as below:

HE'S THE ONE WHO KNOWS US
HE SEES OUR HEART AND HOW WE LIVE OUR LIVES
HE CREATED OUR SHADOW WITH US
THE FOUNDATION OF OUR LIVES
AND THE END
HE SEES ALL SECRETS.

I wonder seriously why some people do things their way rather than God's approved way and still believe that God is on their side. The Bible clearly says in Proverbs 24:23-25,

> "These things also belong to the wise; it is not good to show partiality in judgement. He who says to the wicked, "You are righteous," Him the people will curse; Nations will abhor him. But those who rebuke the wicked will have delight, and good blessing will come upon them."

I have seen Pastors turn the pulpit into their PhD ('Pull him Down, Pull her Down). Someone once said to me that pulpit means where one goes to pull people out of the pit where the devil has pushed them into. Therefore, as Christians, our assignment is not different from what Jesus Christ said He has come to do in Luke 4:18-19:

> "The Spirit of the Lord is upon Me, Because He has anointed Me to preach the gospel to the poor; He has sent Me to heal the broken-hearted, to proclaim liberty to the captives And

recovery of sight to the blind, To set at liberty those who are oppressed; To proclaim the acceptable year of the Lord."

This is Christ's mission, and as His ambassadors and co-labourers, this too should be our focus, pulling people out from pits. God is not pleased with the death of any sinner, but we have received a mandate from Him to help others.

According to Ezekiel 22:30,

"I looked for someone who might rebuild the wall of righteousness that guards the land. I searched for someone to stand in the gap in the wall so I wouldn't have to destroy the land, but I found no one."

The essence of any man's call by God is to ensure that through him, many more would be drawn by God into His kingdom. Anything short of this is a colossal failure in ministry. Whenever I see a ministry or a minister for that matter who is economical about investing in Soul Winning for whatever reasons, I see someone who is selfish. It does not matter how many miracles we may perform; if our focus is not on bringing in others into the kingdom, we are selfish. The duty call should be, "Come taste and see that the Lord is good." However, if we prefer anything else, including mortgage payment for big edifices to demonstrate to people how far we have arrived or how much we have achieved in ministry, then we are to be pitied to say the least, seeing that Matthew 25 should always be at the back of our minds in whatever we do. The Lord is not so much interested in the size of our church buildings as He is in the souls we have ministered to. How much time do we invest in winning souls for Jesus? How much of our budget goes into soul winning? These should be paramount in our hearts at all times.

> *"Remember the word which Moses the servant of the Lord commanded you, saying, "The Lord your God is giving you rest and is giving you this land, Until the Lord has given your brethren rest, as He has given you, and they also have taken possession of the land which the Lord your God is giving them, Then you shall return to the land of your possession and enjoy it, which Moses the Lord's servant gave you on this side of the Jordan toward the sunrise." So they answered Joshua, saying, "All that you command us we will do, and wherever you send us we will go" (Joshua 1:13-16).*

These days it is like most believers choose to do their own things, not caring what the scripture says.

Jonah learnt his lessons the hard way though. He was swallowed by a fish.

Whenever Jonah's name is mentioned anywhere, the first thing that is remembered about him is that he was swallowed and vomited by a fish. That overshadows the fact that he did preach to the people he was sent to at Nineveh. That was a scar.

> "So they picked up Jonah and threw him into the sea, and the sea ceased from its raging. Then the men feared the Lord exceedingly and offered a sacrifice to the Lord and took vows. Now the Lord had prepared a great fish to swallow Jonah. And Jonah was in the belly of the fish three days and three nights. Wherever Jonah's story is told, the first thing that comes to mind is not the assignment he carried out but the fact that he tried to run away initially, and the Lord made his life to face a tempest, and he was swallowed up by a fish, even though he later repented" (Jonah 1:15-17),
>
> "Those who regard worthless idols forsake their own Mercy. But I will sacrifice to you with the voice of thanksgiving; I will pay what I have vowed. Salvation is of the Lord." So the Lord spoke to the fish, and it vomited Jonah onto dry land" (Jonah 2:8-10).
>
> "Now the word of the Lord came to Jonah the second time, saying, "Arise, go to Nineveh,

that great city, and preach to it the message I tell you." So Jonah arose and went to Nineveh, according to the word of the Lord. Now Nineveh was an exceedingly great city, a three-day journey in extent. And Jonah began to enter the city on the first day's walk. Then he cried out and said, "Yet forty days and Nineveh shall be overthrown." So the people of Nineveh believed God, proclaimed a fast, and put on sackcloth, from the greatest to the least of them" (Jonah 3:1-5).

The moment Jonah preached to them, they believed in God. No wonder the Bible says categorically in Romans 10:14,

"How then shall they call on Him in whom they have not believed? And how shall they believe in Him of whom they have not heard? And how shall they hear without a preacher?"

ELIJAH

Elijah was another man who enjoyed a great deal, his work with the Lord. God worked great miracles through him. The Lord stopped the rain from falling on the earth at the word of Elijah.

In James 5:17-18, the Bible says,

> *"Elijah was a man with a nature like ours, and he prayed earnestly that it would not rain, and it did not rain on the land for three years and six months. And he prayed again, and the heaven gave rain, and the earth produced its fruit."*

In 1 Kings 17:1, we read,

> *"And Elijah the Tishbite, of the inhabitants of Gilead, said to Ahab, "As the Lord God of Israelites, before whom I stand, there shall not be dew nor rain these years except at my word."*

The Lord used him to perform a miracle of abundance in the life of a widow; the widow of Zarephath (1 Kings 17:13-16):

> *"And Elijah said to her, "Do not fear; go and do as you have said, but make me a small cake from it first, and bring it to me, and afterward make some for yourself and your son. "For thus says the Lord God of Israel: The bin of flour shall not be used up, nor shall the jar of oil run dry, until the day the Lord sends rain on the earth. So she went and did according to the word of Elijah, and she and he and her household ate for many days. The bin of flour was not used up nor did the jar of oil run dry,*

according to the word of the word of the Lord which He spoke by Elijah."

The Lord also used him to raise the dead (1 Kings 17:17-2):

> *"Now it happened after these things that the son of the woman who owned the house became sick. And his sickness was so serious that there was no breath left in him. So she said to Elijah, "What have I to do with you, O man of God? Have you come to me to bring my sin to remembrance, and to kill my son? And he said to her, "Give me your son." So he took him out of her arms and carried him to the upper room where he was staying, and laid him on his own bed. Then he cried out to the Lord and said, "O Lord my God, have You also brought tragedy on the widow with whom I lodge, by killing her son? And he stretched himself out on the child three times, and cried out to the Lord and said, "O Lord my God, I pray, let this child's soul come back to him." Then the Lord heard the voice of Elijah: and the soul of the child came back to him, and he revived. And Elijah took the child and brought him down from the upper room into the house, and gave him to his mother. And Elijah said, "See, your son lives!" Then the woman said to Elijah, "Now by this I know that you are a man of God and that the word of the Lord in your mouth is the truth."*

The Lord used Elijah to disgrace the prophets of Baal (idol worshippers, 1 Kings 18:40):

> *"And Elijah said to them, "Seize the prophets of Baal! Do not let one of them escape!" So they seized them, and Elijah brought them down to the Brook Kishon and executed them there."*

Elijah enjoyed a high speed. He outran on foot, Ahab who took off long before himself on a chariot (1 Kings 18:45-46).

One would have expected that a man who enjoyed all these uncommon privileges from God would have finished better. Unfortunately, the moment pride entered him, and he began to see himself as being the only prophet who had not bowed to Baal whereas every other one had done so, the Lord said to him that it was time for him to leave the scene because He still had seven thousand in Israel who had not bowed to Baal and every mouth that had not kissed him (1 Kings 19:18).

God asked him to anoint Elisha the son of Shaphat as prophet in his place (1 Kings 19:16). It is true that Elijah was taken up, but he was taken up before his time.

Any man of God, despite the level of relationship they may be enjoying with God, and the barrels of anointing oil they may have on their head, who begins to feel as though they are the best that God can find and use, may be taken away before their time because the Bible tells us that God loves humility.

The Bible says in 2 Chronicles 7:14,

> *"If my people who are called by My name, shall HUMBLE themselves; PRAY; SEEK My face; TURN away from their evil ways, Then the Lord will HEAR from heaven; FORGIVE their sin; and HEAL their land."*

We need to follow God's priority. HUMILITY is the FIRST, and NOT Prayer.

DAVID

David was the man that the Bible described as the man after God's own heart (1 Samuel 13:14).

In fact, God boasted concerning David.

> *"Then God removed Saul and made David their king, about whom He testified, "I have found that David, the son of Jesse, is a man after My own heart, who will carry out all my wishes" (Acts 13:22, ISV).*

After removing Saul, God raised up David as their king. He testified about him:

"I have found David the son of Jesse to be a man after my heart, who will accomplish everything I want him to do."

David only had to follow God's instructions or directives.

Of David, the Bible records in Acts 13:36 (KJV),

"For David, after he had served his own generation according to the will of God, fell asleep, and was laid unto his fathers, and saw corruption."

The NLT puts it this way:

"This is not a reference to David, for after David had done the will of God in his own generation, he died and was buried with his ancestor, and his body decayed."

David found so much favour with God that even when his parents had relegated him to the fields where his assignment was to tender his father's sheep. Samuel sent for him and anointed him as king in place of Saul, even though he was not the eldest son of Jesse. The anointing of God was so much on his life that he even testified that he killed the lion and the bear with his bare hands. When Saul tried to kill him out of envy, God preserved his life by causing the spirit of sleepiness to visit Saul.

However, David got quite a few things wrong in his walk with God, which include the adultery he committed with Uriah's wife and the subsequent killing of her husband (2 Samuel 11). However, the one I believe stood out apart from impregnating Uriah's wife and the killing of her husband, was the fact that he took a census of Israel for a wrong reason. The taking of the census is not a sin, but the motive or the reasons behind it could be. Taking of census in itself was not a sin.

Exodus 30:12 says,

> *"When you take a census of the Israelites to count them, each one must pay a ransom for his soul unto the Lord when you number them so that there be no plague among them when you number them."*

1 Chronicles tell us that Satan, who was against ancient Israel, moved or provoked King David to count his troops.

Satan moved in spiritual warfare against the nation of Israel - not just the king. With his cunning ways, the devil set out to entice David to sin by numbering his army - which is exactly what he did (1 Chronicles 21:1).

2 Samuel 24:1 says,

> *"And the anger of the Lord was kindled against Israel, and he moved David against them to say, Go, number Israel and Judah."*

The above verse in the King James Version Bible tends to give a WRONG understanding to the reader. The 1 Chronicles 21:1 KJV verse quoted earlier and the below scripture quote from the Young's Literal Translation Bible (YLT) offers a more accurate explanation of what transpired.

> *"And the anger of Jehovah addeth to burn against Israel, and an adversary (Satan) moved David about them, saying, "Go, number Israel and Judah" (2 Samuel 24:1, YLT).*

It was Satan that moved David to disobey God. David seems to have been prompted by a feeling of pride and ambitious curiosity. Because he did this to determine his power and to trust in it, it offended God. Of itself, taking a census is not unlawful.

Looking at the Scriptures, we can easily deduce that there is an evil intent in their content. Anytime Satan is involved, you can be sure he intends to get someone to sin! He put the thought in David's mind that if he knew the number of young men under his rule, (meaning those fit for war), he could brag or boast how great a king he was - by the size of his army.

Joab, the commander of David's army, tried to warn him not to number Israel and bring an occasion of punishment to the nation (1 Chronicles 21:2-3).

Because of David's sin, God had to strike Israel (1Chronicles 21:7)

> *"David said to God, "I have sinned greatly because I have done this thing; but now I pray, take away the iniquity of Your servant, for I have done very foolishly" The Lord spoke to Gad, saying, "Go and tell David saying, "Thus says the Lord: "I offer you three things; choose one of them for yourself, that I may do it to you."" So Gad came to David and said to him, choose for yourself, either three years of famine or three months to be defeated by your foes with the sword of your enemies overtaking you, or else for three days the sword of the Lord — the plague in the land with the angel of the Lord destroying throughout all the territory of Israel. Now consider what answer I should take back to Him who sent me" (verses 8-12).*

Even though David enjoyed a privileged place in the heart of the Almighty, he still needed to face the consequences of his disobedience.

In verse 14, the Bible says,

> *"So the Lord sent a plague upon Israel, and seventy thousand men of Israel fell."*

At the end of his reign, David was not allowed to build a temple for the Lord.

1 Chronicles 28:3:

> *"But God said to me, "You must not build a temple to honour My name, for you are a warrior and have shed much blood."*

> *"David's Valedictory Address: David called together all the leaders of Israel—tribal administrators, heads of various governmental operations, military commanders and captains, stewards in charge of the property and livestock belonging to the king and his sons—everyone who held responsible positions in the kingdom. King David stood tall and spoke: "Listen to me, my people: I fully intended to build a permanent structure for the Chest of the Covenant of God, God's footstool. But when I got ready to build it, God said to me, "You may not build a house to honour Me - you have done too much fighting - killed too many people." God chose me out of my family to be king over Israel forever. First, he chose Judah as the lead tribe, then He narrowed it down to my family, and finally He picked me from my father's sons - and God gave me*

many! - He chose my son Solomon to sit on the throne of God's rule over Israel. He went on to say, "Your son Solomon will build my house and my courts; I have chosen him to be my royal adopted son, and I will be to him a father. I will guarantee that his kingdom will last if he continues to be as strong-minded in doing what I command and carrying out my decisions as he is doing now." "And now, in this public place, all Israel looking on and God listening in, as God's people, obey and study every last one of the commandments of your God so that you can make the most of living in this good land and pass it on intact to your children, ensuring a good future." (1 Chronicles 28:1-8, MSG).

Isaiah 1:19 says,

"If you are willing and obedient you will eat the good of the land."

Apostle Paul in his epistle to the Corinthians says in 1 Corinthians 3:9-11,

"For we are God's fellow workers; you are God's field; you are God's building. According to the grace of God which was given to me, as a wise master builder, I have laid the foundation, and another builds on it. But let each one take heed how he builds on it. For no

*other foundation can anyone lay than that
which is laid, which is Jesus Christ."*

Jesus Christ has got His standard and will not
lower it because of anyone. We need to be very careful
how we build.

Man of God, and Woman of God, are you looking
after the sheep with love and care or have you become
draconian in your ways?

Have you set your own standard different from
what the Lord Himself requires? Are you
compassionate enough like Jesus Christ? Have you
placed your businesses over and above the flock?

Listen to me, Solomon says in Proverbs 27:23-27,

> *"Be diligent to know the state of your flocks,
> and attend to your herds; for riches are not
> forever, nor does a crown endure to all
> generations. When the hay is removed, and the
> tender grass shows itself, and the herbs of the
> mountains are gathered in, the lambs will
> provide your clothing, and the goats the price
> of a field, you shall have enough goats' milk for
> your food, for food of your household, and the
> nourishment of your maidservants."*

Paul writes in Acts 20:28-31,

> *"Therefore take heed to yourselves and to all
> the flock, among which the Holy Spirit has*

made you overseers, to shepherd the church of God which He purchased with His own blood. For I know this, that after my departure savage wolves will come in among you, not sparing the flock. Also from among yourselves men will rise up, speaking perverse things, to draw away the disciples after themselves. Therefore, watch and remember that for three years I did not cease to warn every one night and day with tears."

How we do the work of God matters a lot to God. We can see this clearly from what the Bible says in John 6:27-29,

"Do not labour for the food which perishes, but for the food which endures to everlasting life, which the Son of Man will give you because God the Father has set His seal on Him." Then they said to him, "what shall we do, that we may work the works of God?" Jesus answered and said to them, "This is the work of God, that you believe in Him whom He sent."

What was Jesus sent to do? In Luke 4:18-19,

"Jesus says, "The Spirit of the Lord is upon Me, Because He has anointed Me to preach the gospel to the poor; He has sent Me to heal the broken-hearted, To proclaim liberty to the captives And recovery of sight to the blind, To

set at liberty those who are oppressed; To proclaim the acceptable year of the Lord.""

In Luke 19:10, Jesus says,

"For the Son of Man has come to seek and to save that which was lost."

The Bible says in Deuteronomy 15:11,

"For the poor will never cease in the land; therefore I command you saying; "You must open your hand wide to your brother, to your poor and your needy, in your land."

Verses 14-15 say,

"You shall supply him liberally from your flock, from your threshing floor, and from your winepress, from what the Lord your God has blessed you with, you shall give to him. You shall remember that you were a slave in the land of Egypt, and the Lord your God redeemed you; therefore I command you this thing today."

Often, I am surprised the way Christians interpret what Jesus said in Matthew 25:29-30,

"For to everyone who has, more will be given, and he will have abundance; but from him who does not have, even what he has will be taken away." And cast the unprofitable servant into

the outer darkness. There will be weeping and
gnashing of teeth."

To many believers, the above scripture only refer to
wealth accumulation, or money, whereas what that
scripture is saying is explained better in the following
verses. Let us see the subsequent verses:

"When the Son of Man comes in His glory,
and all the holy angels with Him, then He will
sit on the throne of His glory. All the nations
will be gathered before Him, and he will
separate them one from another, as a shepherd
divides his sheep from the goats. And He will
set the sheep on His right hand, but the goats
on the left. Then the King will say to those on
His right hand, "Come, you blessed of My
Father, inherit the kingdom prepared for you
from the foundation of the world: "For I was
hungry, and you gave Me food; I was thirsty,
and you gave Me drink; I was a stranger, and
you took Me in.; I was naked, and you clothed
Me; I was sick, and you visited Me, I was in
prison, and you came to Me." Then the
righteous will answer Him, saying, "Lord,
when did we see You hungry and feed You, or
thirsty and give You drink? When did we see
You a stranger and take You in, or naked and
clothe You? Or when did we see You sick, or
in prison, and come to You?" "And the King
will answer and say to them, "Assuredly I say

to you, inasmuch as you did it to one of the least of these My brethren, you did it to Me." Then He will also say to those on the left hand, "Depart from Me, you cursed, into the everlasting fire prepared for the devil and his angels; for I was hungry, and you gave Me no food; I was thirsty, and you gave Me no drink; I was a stranger, and you did not take Me in, naked, and you did not clothe Me, sick and in prison and you did not visit Me." Then they will answer Him, saying, "Lord, when did we see You hungry or thirsty or a stranger or naked or sick or in prison, and did not minister to you? Then He will answer them saying, "Assuredly, I say to you, inasmuch as you did not do it to one of the least of these, you did not do it to Me." "And these will go away into everlasting punishment, but the righteous into eternal life" (verses 31-46).

Brethren, it does matter how we do the work. Jesus Christ died for the whole world as a result of love (John 3:16). Jesus says in John 15:13,

"Greater love has no one than this than to lay down one's life for his friends."

To be called Christian means being Christlike, and being Christlike means having Christ's attributes and Jesus's attitude. In Acts of the Apostles 11:26, the Bible records that His disciples were first referred to as

Christians in Antioch. In Acts 4:13, the Bible also records that those people who saw His disciples realised without anyone telling them that they had been with Jesus.

As a Christian, has His life genuinely rubbed off on you? Have you got time for lost souls? Is your love for your neighbour genuine? Have you added what Jesus did not add to His teachings? Where is your emphasis? On souls or material things? Have you restructured scriptures to justify your greed for money? None of these escapes His attention.

Psalm 139:7-12 says:

> *"Where can I go from Your Spirit? Or where can I flee from Your presence? If I ascend into heaven, You are there; If I make my bed in hell, behold You are there. If I take the wings of the morning and dwell in the uttermost parts of the sea, Even there Your hand shall lead me, and Your right hand shall hold me; Indeed, the darkness shall not hide from you, but the night shines as the day; the darkness and the light are both alike to You."*

It does not matter how much privilege any man enjoys in the heart of God, every act of disobedience to God attracts a penalty and leaves a scar

SAMSON

One of the things that Samson is easily remembered by is his dealings with Delilah, but very rarely do people even consider that he was a man for whom God had great plans (Judges 13:1-5).

Samson was a man called by God for a specific purpose. He was brought into the world to be a Deliverer. The children of Israel did evil in the sight of the Lord, and the Lord delivered them into the hands of the Philistines forty years. There was a man named Manoah whose wife was barren. The angel of the Lord appeared to her and told her that she was going to have a son who would deliver Israel from the hands of the Philistines.

In Judges, God gave specific instructions concerning that Deliverer that was to come through Manoah's wife's womb.

We know that God has a specific assignment for all of His creatures. Nobody is here by accident. It is written in Jeremiah 1:4-5,

> *"Then the word of the Lord came unto me, saying, Before I formed you in the womb, I knew you; and before you came out from the womb, I sanctified you, and I ordained you a prophet unto the nations."*

To fulfil his calling, Samson only needed to adhere to the plans of God for his life. In Judges 13:24-25, the Bible records,

> *"And the woman bare a son, and called his name Samson: and the child grew, and the Lord blessed him. And the Spirit of the Lord began to move him at times in the camp of Dan between Zorah and Eshtaol."*

Samson enjoyed some great privileges from God. First of all, God gave him a plan to deal with the Philistines who at that time were lording it over Israel. God put the desire in him for a woman from Timnath who was a Philistine. That was strange to the parents, and they tried to dissuade him from having eyes for an "enemy" (Judges 14:1-4).

Samson tore a lion into shreds with his bare hands (Judges 14:5-9).

Samson killed thirty people at Ashkelon within one go (Judges 14:19).

Samson was tied with two new cords by three thousand men on the rock of Etam and was brought to Lehi, where the Spirit of the Lord came mightily upon him and burnt off the bands from his hands, and as he was freed, he was able to perform all that he could not up until then. He slew thousands with the jawbone of an axe (Judges 15:11-17).

Samson also enjoyed the miracle of having God bring water from the hollow of the jawbone for him to drink (Judges 15:19).

Samson carried the doors of the city gate and the two posts on his shoulders and went away, thereby escaping from those who were waiting to kill him (Judges 16:3).

Samson judged Israel for twenty years (Judges 15:20).

Everything was pointing to the direction of one who was going to fulfil his calling according to the plans and purposes of God Almighty. However, it is not how one starts off that matters but how one finishes.

What Samson did not acknowledge was that none of these conquests was by his might. The Holy Spirit was behind every of his triumph.

The Bible says in Zechariah 4:6, "It is not by power and it is not by might, but by the power of the Holy Spirit. Whenever a man of God starts relying on their strength, it means that they have lost it already.

Samson had a great anointing that was sufficient to help him fulfil his calling and finish well, but his character was what brought him down.

Judges 16:20 says of Samson,

> *"Then she cried out, "Samson! The Philistines have come to capture you!" When he woke up, he thought, "I will do as before and shake myself free." But he did not realise that the Lord had left him.""*

> *"So the Philistines captured him and gouged out his eyes. They took him to Gaza, where he was bound with bronze chains and forced to grind grain in the prison" (Judges 16:21).*

As Matthew 6:22 says,

> *"Your eye is a lamp that provides light for your body. When your eye is good, your whole body is filled with light."*

My Pastor says, "In the absence of God's glory is the abundance of the devil's gory."

Unfortunately, the Spirit of the Lord has left many "Men of God", but God still leaves them in their position of ministry. Like I said earlier, God is the only employer who will give a man the sack and still leave them working. May God's mercy prevail in our lives.

Concerning Samson, my Pastor would say, "When the loins of the powerful are exposed, the lion in the mighty is disposed."

Chapter Eight
PRIDE IN THE BODY OF CHRIST

It baffles me so much to what extent pride has crept into the Body of Christ. Christians are no longer called brethren. There is in the Church now, if not Caste system, Class system. Which God are we serving now? Surely, this cannot be the same Jesus, an epitome of humility whom the Bible described in Matthew 26:45-54,

> *"Then He came to His disciples and said to them, "Are you still sleeping and resting? Behold, the hour is at hand, and the Son of Man is being betrayed into the hands of sinners. "Rise, let us be going. See, My betrayer is at hand." And while He was still speaking, behold, Judas, one of the twelve, with a great multitude with swords and clubs, came from the chief priests and elders of the people. Now His betrayer had given them a sign, saying, "WHOMEVER I KISS, HE IS THE ONE; Seize Him." Immediately he went up to Jesus and said," Greetings, Rabbi!" and kissed*

Him. But Jesus said to him, "Friend, why have you come? Then they came and laid hands on Jesus and took Him. And suddenly, one of those who were with Jesus stretched out his hand and drew his sword, struck the servant of the high priest, and cut off his ear." But Jesus said to him, "Put your sword in its place, for all who take the sword will perish by the sword. Or do you think that I cannot now pray to My Father, and He will provide Me with more than twelve legions of angels? "How then could the Scripture be fulfilled, that it must happen thus? In that hour Jesus said to the multitudes, "Have you come out as against a robber, with swords and clubs to take Me? I sat daily with you, teaching in the temple, and you did not seize Me. "But all this was done that the Scriptures of the prophets might be fulfilled." Then all the disciples forsook Him and fled."

Jesus was so ORDINARY and so down to earth in His dealings with his disciples that it could only take a kiss from Judas to show His abductors who He was. Whatever has happened to humility in the Body of Christ.

If as joint-heirs we are not even seeing our fellow Christians as our equal, then how do we look at the unsaved? Why are we complaining that they do not come to our events?

When you receive Jesus, you have just come into the fellowship of humiliation, rejection and persecution. 2 Timothy 3:12 says, "Yes, and all who desire to live godly in Christ Jesus will suffer persecution.

Brethren, can God indeed boast about us and say that His boasting in us has proved right? Or has His standard suddenly reduced because of grace?

Romans 6:1 says,

> "Shall we continue in sin because grace abounds? God forbid."

In other words, those who use their position to oppress other people, most especially those under them, simply because they wrongly deceive themselves that they have control of the world, should be ready to face the consequences that must surely come with such behaviour. It is not surprising therefore why the Bible says in Colossians 4:1,

> "Masters, give your bondservants what is just and fair, knowing that you also have a Master in heaven."

God is very interested in how human beings especially His followers treat other human beings.

It is written in Philippians 2:5,

> *"Let this mind be in you which was in Christ Jesus."*

In Christ is the mind of love; love for sinners. He was compassionate. That was what made Him give up His place in exchange for our own. It was love that made Him go to the Cross. Bible says in Romans 5:8,

> *"While we were yet sinners, Christ died for us." John 3:16 records, "For God so loved the world that He gave His only begotten Son, so that whoever believes in Him will not perish but have everlasting life."*

We are Christians only if we are like Christ.

As Christians, we are required to love just precisely like Christ. This is the greatest evidence of our fellowship with Him. In John 13:34-35, Jesus said,

> *"A new commandment I give to you, that you love one another as I have loved you, that you also love one another. By this, all will know that you are My disciples if you have love for one another."*

This means that the consequence of not loving that way means that the person automatically is not a disciple. There are no two ways about it. Love can only be demonstrated rather than preached, and its demonstration is the way 1 Corinthians 13 explains it.

PRIDE AND MINISTRY

Pride has and will continue to short-circuit people's ministry and lives. God hates it like leprosy.

Sometimes I have wondered whether some ministers of the Gospel have thought of the reason why Paul wrote in 2 Corinthians 12:2-10,

> *"I know a man in Christ who fourteen years ago, whether in the body I do not know, or whether out of the body I do not know, God knows - such a one was caught up to the third heaven. And I know such a man-whether in the body or out of the body, I do not know, God knows how he was caught up into Paradise and heard inexpressible words, which it is not lawful for a man to utter. Of such a one I will boast; yet of myself, I will not boast, except in my infirmities. For though I might desire to boast, I will not be a fool; for I will speak the truth. But I refrain, lest anyone should think of me above what he sees me to be or hears from me. Lest I should be exalted above measure by the abundance of the revelations, a thorn in the flesh was given to me, a messenger of Satan to buffet me, lest I be exalted above measure. Concerning this thing, I pleaded with the Lord*

three times that it might depart from me. And He said to me, "My grace is sufficient for you, for My strength is made perfect in weakness." Therefore most gladly I will rather boast in my infirmities, that the power of Christ may rest upon me. Therefore I take pleasure in infirmities, in reproaches, in needs, in persecutions, in distresses, for Christ's sake. For when I am weak, then I am strong."

When some people receive spiritual revelations, they become very proud of themselves such that if God does not stop them in time, pride might destroy them. There is nothing a man will ever receive unless it is given. Why do we behave as though we did not receive these gifts? Why would a man allow the devil to deceive him and make him think he had become "larger than life?"

Pride is the quickest lane to hellfire. Many people are operating in the gift they got from God, but they are no longer in touch with the God of the gift. The Bible says in Romans 11:29,

"For the gifts and calling of God are irrevocable."

For instance, if I buy a tie or a shirt and give to a friend and eventually stop speaking with the person, will I take back the gifts? Obviously no. The person may still be showing the gifts to our common friends and saying I gave him those gifts. That does not mean we are still friends. It does not matter how loud one sings the song "I am a friend of God, He calls me friend." Does He call us His friends or have we long ceased being His friends and are only just displaying His gifts?

Lucifer was the Choirmaster or Worship leader in heaven. Everything that could produce a melody was inside of his being. When he lost his place in God's presence, the Bible did not say that the gift of singing was taken from him. That is why he can easily manifest himself in some choirs in the church.

Some Christians, particularly men and women of God, have carried themselves with such arrogance as though they have become the almighty God themselves. May I remind them that they are not God and that our God is a jealous God. The ambassador of any country to another country may enjoy the status of the president of his country in his new territory, but he is not the president.

Jesus says, in Matthew 23:9-14,

> *"And don't address anyone here on earth as "Father," for only God in heaven is your spiritual Father. And don't let anyone call you "Teacher," for you have only one teacher, the*

Messiah. The greatest among you must be a servant. But those who exalt themselves will be humbled, and those who humble themselves will be exalted. What sorrow awaits you teachers of religious law and you Pharisees. Hypocrites! For you shut the door of the Kingdom of Heaven in the people's faces. You won't go in yourselves, and you don't let others enter either."

"Fight for your own salvation with fear and with trembling" (Philippians 2:12).

"Do you think that I like to see wicked people die? Says the Sovereign Lord. Of course not! I want them to turn from their wicked ways and live. However, if righteous people turn from their righteous behaviour and start doing sinful things and act like other sinners, should they be allowed to live? No, of course not! All their righteous acts will be forgotten, and they will die for their sins. Yet you say, "The Lord isn't doing what is right!" Listen to Me, O people of Israel. Am I the one not doing what is right, or is it you? When righteous people turn from their righteous behaviour and start doing sinful things, they will die for it. Yes, they will die because of their sinful deeds" (Ezekiel 18:23-26, NLT)

From what we see here, the will of the Almighty is that man shall live and not die, just as He says in Deuteronomy 30:19. Death comes to a man as a consequence of man's disobedience

Proverbs 11:18 (ESV) puts it this way:

> *"The wicked earns deceptive wages, but one who sows righteousness gets a sure reward."*

To serve God and finish well in ministry, having a good character is as essential as being anointed. To succeed in Ministry, one needs more than anointing. A lot of Christians deceive themselves by believing that all there is to prove that God is with them is when signs and wonders are happening in their ministry. No sir. Those are gifts, and the Bible tells us that the gifts and calling of God are without repentance (Romans 11:29). Our gifts at best can make way for us and cause us to sit with great men (Proverbs 18:16).

However, the ingredients we need to finish well are called fruits. Matthew 7:16, 20 say that we are known by fruits the fruits we bear. Galatians 5:22 enumerates the virtues that we need to show forth in our lives to finish well. The Bible calls them the FRUIT of the Spirit.

The gifts you have cannot help you to heaven, but the fruit you demonstrate is what will guide you into heaven at the last breath. Many believers think that because of the gifts they have that heaven is secured already, but I know that Jesus says in Matthew 7:21-23,

> *"Not everyone who says to Me, Lord, Lord, shall enter the kingdom of heaven, but he who does the will of My Father in heaven. Many will say to Me in that day, Lord, Lord, have we not prophesied in Your name, cast out demons in Your name, and done many wonders in Your name? And then I will declare to them, I never knew you; depart from Me, you who practice lawlessness!"*

There are some common factors shared by those who didn't end well; those who left scars that trail them even after they have left the scene.

They did not trust the very people they developed for succession

Even today, those leaders who are not finishing well seem always to be dissatisfied with who succeeds them, always as if they are looking for and unable to find a clone for themselves.

They fought over things which were just not that important.

They majored on the minors, and those who were the objects of that constant attention knew another "concern" was just around the corner. The Bible says in Matthew 6:33,

> *"And seek you first the kingdom of God and His righteousness, and everything else shall be added unto you.*

In Mark 1:35-37, it is written that Jesus went very early in the morning to seek the face of His Father, and when Peter and others who were with him found Him, they said to him, "all men seek you." When we look for Him, everything else will look for us. It is a principle that cannot fail.

Their identities were too connected to their movement and ministry

When you hear leaders who keep saying "my church, my church", you have seen a man that would most likely falter at the finishing line. Jesus says it is His church (Matthew 16:18) and that we are just co-labourers with Him. 1 Corinthians 3:9 says,

> *"For we are co-labourers in God's service; you are God's field, you are God's building."*

2 Corinthians 6:1 says,

> *"As God's co-labourers we urge you not to receive God's grace in vain."*

The church isn't yours, so please stop behaving as though it were your property where you can treat people anyhow you like otherwise there is the risk of not finishing without a scar.

We ought to be sharpening one another as iron sharpens iron. We ought to look at the examples of those who have gone on before us (1 Corinthians 10:1-24), and then we also need to take a look in the mirror and examine ourselves (2 Corinthians 13:5)

Whenever a believer starts seeing anyone as inferior to himself, he is already in disobedience to the command.

In John 13:34-35, Jesus says,

> *"A new commandment I give to you, that you love one another as I have loved you, that you also love one another. By this, all will know that you are My disciples if you have love one for another."*

Are you encouraging and supporting any form of tribalism in the church of God? You have already left a scar because it should not be so. The Bible says we are all sons and daughters of God, hence brothers and sisters.

If you are discriminating and showing favouritism in the church of God, you are causing a division in the

body of Christ and in the words of Jesus Christ
Himself in Matthew 12:25 and Mark 3:25,

> *"If a house is divided against itself, that house
> cannot stand.*

According to the word of God in Ecclesiastes 7:8,

> *"Better is the end of a thing than the beginning
> thereof."*

Is your ministry showing great signs and wonders
today? How would it end? How would you want to
be remembered? What legacy are you leaving
behind?

It is written of our God in Psalm 86:8-12,

> *"Among the gods, there is none like You, O
> Lord; Nor are there any works like Your works.
> All nations whom You have made shall come
> and worship before You, O Lord, And glorify
> Your name. For You are great, and do
> wondrous things; You alone are God. Teach me
> Your way, O Lord; I will walk in Your truth;
> Unite my heart to fear Your name. I will praise
> You, O Lord my God, with all my heart, and I
> will glorify Your name forevermore."*

It does not matter who; every knee must bow to our
God, and every tongue must confess that Jesus is the
Lord to the glory of God.

Nebuchadnezzar did not seem to understand that therefore he provoked God to anger (Daniel 3) by making an image of gold and commanded that everyone must worship such an image, and whoever does not fall down and worship shall be cast into the midst of a burning fiery furnace. Three Hebrew boys Shadrach, Meshach and Abed-Nego refused to bow to and worship the golden image and told him that the God of heaven whom they served would deliver them from the burning fiery furnace should they be thrown inside it. He gave the command, and they were bound and thrown into the furnace, and not only were they not burnt, the men who threw them into the furnace died. When the King saw that the three boys were walking about freely inside the furnace and he also observed that a fourth man that looked like the Son of God was there with them, he said this (Daniel 3:29-30),

> *"Therefore I make a decree that any people, nation, or language which speaks anything amiss against the God of Shadrach, Meshach and Abed-Nego shall be cut in pieces, and their houses shall be made an ash heap; because there is no other God who can deliver like this."*

Then the King promoted Shadrach, Meshach and Abed-Nego in the province of Babylon.

Anyone who would not humble himself before our God, irrespective of what they do for Him, will be humiliated by Him because He alone is God.

One would think that after this experience the King would have realised that our God is indeed a jealous God, and would correct himself. However, he still had pride inside. The Bible records in Daniel 4:28-37,

> *"All this came upon King Nebuchadnezzar. At the end of the twelve months, he was walking about the royal palace of Babylon. The King spoke, saying, "Is not this great Babylon, that I have built for a royal dwelling by my mighty power and for the honour of my majesty?" While the word was still in the king's mouth, a voice fell from heaven: "King Nebuchadnezzar, to you it is spoken: the kingdom has departed from you And they shall drive you from men, and your dwelling shall be with the beasts of the field. They shall make you eat grass like oxen, and seven times shall pass over you until you know that the Most High rules in the kingdom of men, and gives it to whomever He chooses." That very hour the word was fulfilled concerning Nebuchadnezzar; he was driven from men and ate grass like oxen; his body was wet with the dew of heaven till his hair had grown like eagles' feathers and his nails like birds' claws. And at the end of the time, I, Nebuchadnezzar,*

lifted my eyes to heaven, and my understanding returned to me; and I blessed the Most High and praised and honoured Him who lives forever: For His dominion is an everlasting dominion. And his kingdom is from generation to generation. All the inhabitants of the earth are reputed as nothing; He does according to his will in the army of heaven and among the inhabitants of the earth. No one can restrain His hand or say to him, "What have You done?" At the same time my reason returned to me, and for the glory of my kingdom, my honour and glory returned to me. My counsellors and nobles resorted to me, I was restored to my kingdom, and excellent majesty was added to me. Now I, Nebuchadnezzar, praise and extol and honour the King of heaven, all of whose works are truth, and his ways justice. And those who walk in pride He is able to put down."

Little wonder why the Bible says in Proverbs 29:23,

"A man's pride will bring him low, but the humble in spirit will retain honour."

The surest way to lose honour is pride. Pride is the gateway to dishonour. Unfortunately, many have fallen short of God's glory due to pride, and as I said earlier, the devil wants to tarnish as many testimonies as possible in order to take some people to hell with him. Most believers have missed it already without realising it. Nebuchadnezzar in Daniel 3:29 had decreed that nobody should serve any other God except the God of the three Hebrew boys, yet he had the spirit of pride. It goes to say that some people may actually be in church, profess with their mouth that there is no other God but Jehovah, yet their attitude will not show in any way that God is the One who gives them the power to preach well, or prophecy, or make money or whatever they have achieved.

The Bible's commands are not voluntary but that we should obey to the letters. For example, when the Bible says, "Wives submit to your own husbands, and husbands love your wife," it does not discriminate. The Bible also admonishes children to honour their parents and warns parents against provoking their children to wrath knowing that everyone who fails in this will have a question to answer before our Lord on the day of judgement. Often, some Pastors maltreat their spouses and terrorise both their biological and spiritual children, hiding under the cloak of "Touch not my anointed and do my Prophets no harm." This already makes them instruments in the devil's hands even though they may be ministering from the pulpit. It is essential that everyone threads carefully in other to make heaven. Apostle Paul said in 1 Corinthians 9:27,

"I discipline my flesh so that after I have preached to others and brought them to salvation, I myself becomes a castaway."

It is very easy to minister to others under a powerful anointing, with signs and wonders following and still not be in the good books of our God. Jesus says it very clearly in Matthew 7:21-27,

"Not everyone who says to Me, "Lord, Lord, shall enter the kingdom of heaven, but he who does the will of My Father in heaven. Many will say to Me in that day: "Lord, Lord, have we not prophesied in Your name, cast out demons in Your name, and done many wonders in Your name?" And then I will declare to them, "I never knew you; depart from Me, you who practice lawlessness." Therefore, whoever hears these sayings of mine, and does them, I will liken him to a wise man who built his house on the rock: "and the rain descended, the floods came, and the winds blew and beat on that house, and it did not fall, for it was founded on the rock. "But everyone who hears these sayings of mine, and does not do them, will be like a foolish man who built his house on the sand: "and the rain descended, the floods came, and the winds blew and beat on that house, and it fell. And great was its fall."

The fact that you work miracles is not an excuse to live the way you want to, treating everyone else as though they are insignificant. Christ Jesus went to the Cross for every human being. God, the Bible says, is not pleased with the death of the sinner. He saved us that He may use us to reach the unsaved with His love and compassion so that they too may be saved. Anyone living their lives as though the Great Commission is not for them is in the wrong. It is a command and should be obeyed to the letter. That Commission says, "GO" into all the world and make disciples of all nations." Even if your title is G.O., it still means "GO."

In whatever position of importance you find yourself in life, always remember that without the grace of God you cannot do anything. John 3:27 clearly says that "A man can receive nothing except it be given to him from heaven."

In 1 Corinthians 4:7 it is written,

> *"For who makes you differ from another. And what do you have that you did not receive? Now if you indeed receive it, why do you boast as if you had not received it?" If you have been very full of yourself and believing that why you are where you are is because you are very smart, I would advise you to repent because*

Solomon, the wisest man who ever lived, said in Ecclesiastes 9:11,

"I returned and saw under the sun that the race is not to the swift, nor the battle to the strong, nor bread to the wise, nor riches to men of understanding, nor favour to men of skill, but time and chance happen to them all."

In one of his epistles to the Romans, Paul wrote,

"So then it is not of him who wills, nor of him who runs, but of God who shows mercy. For the scripture says to Pharaoh, "For this very purpose I have raised you up, that I may show My power in you, and that My name may be declared in all the earth" (Romans 9:16-17).

He was quoting what God said to Pharaoh in Exodus,

"But indeed for this purpose I have raised you up, that I may show My power in you, and that My name may be declared in all the earth" (Exodus 9:16).

Chapter Nine
JUDAS IN MINISTRY

*"Judas the son of James, and Judas Iscariot who
also became a traitor" (Luke 6:16).*

Luke listed the twelve Apostles of Jesus Christ.
When he got to Judas Iscariot, he identified
him as the Apostle who became a traitor. So as
Christian, what are you becoming or turning to? Judas
was an Apostle who became a traitor. This was a man
who had followed Jesus ministry for three and a half
years, seen all the great miracles of healings and
deliverances. This was a man who had been mightily
used by God to heal the sick, raise the dead, cleanse
the leper and cast out devils (Matthew 10:8). He saw
all the great miracles, signs and wonders, yet he had a
character flaw, a moral weakness. The Bible states that
even though God was using him, Judas was a thief
(John 12:6). He used to pilfer the money box. It is very
important to note that Jesus allowed a thief to carry
the money bag. Sometimes we think the Lord is going

to challenge us on every issue, but there are times His silence about our repeated sin is His rebuke. Judas knew he was doing wrong, but since Jesus did not directly confront him, he minimised the severity of his iniquity. Maybe, he reasoned that if his iniquity were truly bad, Jesus would not still be using him to do miracles.

My dear brothers and sisters, that anger, un-forgiveness, bitterness, bad attitude, bad behaviour, and offence, can cause you to degenerate into someone else you never intended to become. That in itself is a scar. Receive the grace, therefore, to search your heart and begin to get rid of any hidden tendencies of becoming someone you never set out to become on this journey with the Lord. Shed those weights. Hebrews 12:1 says,

> "Therefore we also, since we are surrounded by so great a cloud of witnesses, let us lay aside every weight and the sin which so easily ensnares us, and let us run with endurance the race that is set before us."

Greed for wealth is one of those weights. I once learnt of some Pastors in Italy and some other places, who would undertake a fast and pray for people who travelled to get hard drugs whenever they travelled, so they would arrive safely with the drugs, and once they arrived safely, would compensate the Pastors with huge gifts ranging from money to vehicles for their prayers and fasting. I ask whom they believed answered those prayers. Who did they fast for?

Zechariah 7:4-5 says,

> *"Then the word of the Lord of hosts came to me, saying, "Say to all the people of the land, and to the priests: "When you fasted and mourned in the fifth and seventh years, did you really fast for Me - for Me?"*

Child of God, wealth and fame should not be your aim in the ministry; else you might bow to the devil and lose your place in heaven. You were called to make disciples for Christ, not to make money nor a name for yourself.

Jesus says in Mark 8:36-37,

> *"For what shall it profit a man if he gains the whole world and loses his own soul? Or what will a man give in exchange for his soul?"*

I remember when an "evangelist" kept pestering me that she wanted me to invite her to come and minister in my programme. She kept bothering me until I had to agree that she should come and preach about soul winning as I had a programme on Evangelism. Was I surprised when she asked me how much the Church was going to pay her for coming? It was evident to me immediately that she was not interested in anything than what she was going to get as "remuneration." I told her that I was shocked to hear her say that, to which she responded that she charges money to preach the Gospel. I reminded her that my Bible says in Matthew 10:8, "Freely you receive, and freely you give." She looked for every scripture to justify her greed for money, and I told her that the Bible says in Matthew 10:40-42 that "Whosoever blesses a man of God, out of their own free will, shall not lose their reward."

It is wrong when Christ's representatives have to charge money in other to preach the Good News. Many people are in Ministry because of money.

1 Timothy 6:6-14 says,

> "Now godliness with contentment is great gain. For we brought nothing into this world, and it is certain we can carry nothing out. And having food and clothing, with these we shall be content. But those who desire to be rich fall into temptation and a snare, and into many foolish and harmful lusts which drown men in destruction and perdition. For the love of money is a root of all kinds of evil, for which some have strayed from the faith in their greediness and pierced themselves through

with many sorrows. But you, O man of God, flee these things and pursue righteousness, godliness, faith, love, patience, gentleness. Fight the good fight of faith, lay hold on eternal life, to which you were also called and have confessed in the presence of many witnesses. I urge you in the sight of God who gives life to all things, and before Christ Jesus who witnessed the good confession before Pontius Pilate, that you keep this commandment without spot, blameless until our Lord Jesus Christ's appearing."

Verses 17-20 says,

"Command those who are rich in this present age not to be haughty, nor to trust in uncertain riches but in the living God, who gives us richly all things to enjoy, storing up for themselves a good foundation for the time to come, that they may lay hold on eternal life. O Timothy! Guard what was committed to your trust, avoiding the profane babblings and contradictions of what is falsely called knowledge by professing it some have strayed concerning the faith. Grace be with you. Amen."

Gehazi, Prophet Elisha's servant, brought leprosy upon himself and his descendants forever because of his greed for money. This is a perpetual scar.

In 2 Kings 5:14-17, we read,

"So he went down and dipped seven times in the Jordan, according to the saying of the man of God; and his flesh was restored like the flesh of a little child, and he was clean. And he returned to the man of God, he and all his aides, and came and stood before him (Elisha); and he said, "Indeed, now I know that there is no God in all the earth, except in Israel; now, therefore, please take a gift from your servant." But he said, "As the Lord lives, before whom I stand, I will receive nothing." And he urged him to take it, but he refused. So Naaman said, "Then, if not, please let your servant be given two mule-loads of earth; for your servant will no longer offer either burnt offering or sacrifice to other gods, but to the Lord."

Verses 20-27 concludes,

"But Gehazi, the servant of Elisha the man of God, said, "Look, my master has spared Naaman this Syrian, while not receiving from his hands what he brought; but as the Lord lives, I will run after him and take something from him. So Gehazi pursued Naaman. When Naaman saw him running after him, he got down from the chariot to meet him, and said, "Is it well?" And he said, "All is well. My master has sent me, saying, "Indeed, just now two young men of the sons of the prophets have

come to me from the mountains of Ephraim. Please give them a talent of silver and two changes of garments." So Naaman said, "Please, take two talents." And he urged him, and bound two talents of silver in two bags, with two changes of garments, and handed them to two of his servants; and they carried them on ahead of him. When he came to the citadel, he took them from their hand, and stored them away in the house; then he let them go, and they departed. Now he went in and stood before his master. Elisha said to him, "Where did you go, Gehazi?" And he said, "Your servant did not go anywhere." Then he said to him, "Did not my heart go with you when the man turned back from his chariot to meet you? Is it time to receive clothing, olive groves and vineyards, sheep and oxen, male and female servants? Therefore the leprosy of Naaman shall cling to you and your descendants forever." And he went out from his presence leprous, as white as snow."

What a poor ending!

Elisha had received a double portion of Elijah's anointing, and logically Gehazi was meant to perform twice as much as his own master did, but he ended up badly because of one error of judgement. There is an absolute need to be very careful in our walk with the

Lord because although our God is a merciful God, He is also a Consuming Fire.

Chapter Ten
ARISE, YOU CAN DO IT!

Now it does not matter to God how many times you may have failed, faltered or even fallen in your walk with Him. He is the God who makes available to us ways of reconciling with Him so that we will not miss the ultimate destination which is heaven. He is the God of a second chance. You may have been struggling with the spirit of pride in your life and ministry; the Lord does not want you to serve Him and end up in hell because of pride. He wants you to make heaven at the end of this sojourn on earth.

Apostle Paul was so heaven conscious that he said in 1 Corinthians 9:27,

> *"But I discipline my body and bring it into subjection, lest when I have preached to others, I myself should become disqualified."*

What a tragedy that would be? Be bold and repent. That precisely is what our Lord desires.

The Bible says in Ezra 10:4,

> "Arise for this matter is your responsibility. We also are with you. Be of good courage, and do it."

You may have failed many times, but arise. The angels of God are with you to help you. God does not want you to finish in hell. He knows that the devil wants to take as many believers as possible with him, so would use every trick to deceive many. However, our God has made an eternal provision of reconciliation with Him through the shed blood of the Lamb of God, Jesus Christ the righteous. Don't wallow in self-pity.

Someone once said that the true meaning of 'FAILURE' after all is:

FIRST
ATTEMPT
IN
LEARNING
UNDER
REAL
ENVIRONMENT

Failure is an opportunity to do better next time; so arise and don't beat up yourself.

All that the Lord desires is godly repentance.

"For the kind of sorrow God wants us to experience leads us away from sin and results in salvation. There's no regret for that kind of sorrow. But worldly sorrow, which lacks repentance, results in spiritual death. Just see what this godly sorrow produced in you! Such earnestness, such concern to clear yourselves, such indignation, such alarm, such longing to see me, such zeal, and such a readiness to punish wrong. You showed that you have done everything to make things right" (2 Corinthians 7:10, NLT).

Yes, it does not matter how often one may have failed in their walk with God, His grace to make amends is always available. He wants us to make a complete "U" turn since this grace is not a license to continually live our lives the way we desire. This grace is not to make us continue to live in sin.

Romans 6:1-2 says,

"What shall we say then? Shall we continue in sin that grace may abound? Certainly not!"

Some Christians have unconsciously allowed praise singers and sycophants to ruin their ministry, and my advice is this:

Often, people remain down after a fall, whereas the will of God is that we get up and continue the journey. Joseph advised his brothers to forgive themselves because he had forgiven them. It is not uncommon to see people who are still living with a sense of guilt even after they have been forgiven by the Lord. That is called pride. We should trust God enough to believe that we have been forgiven when He says so. We should be humble enough to understand that even though we are Christians, we are not Christ. We are Christ's ambassadors. We are His representatives here on earth. The ambassador of a nation may represent the President in every capacity in that nation, but that does not suddenly make him the president.

It does not matter where you are with God or what you have done for him, "Don't be impressed by money, followers, degrees and titles. Rather, be impressed by kindness, integrity, humility and generosity" (Public Domain). In these things is the Lord glorified.

God says in Malachi 2:1-9,

> *"And now, O Priests, this commandment is for you. If you will not hear, and if you will not take it to heart, to give glory to My name, says the Lord of hosts, I will send a curse upon you, and I will curse your blessings. Yes, I have cursed them already, because you do not take it to heart. Behold, I will rebuke your descendants and spread refuse on your faces, the refuse of your solemn feasts; and one will*

take you away with it. Then you shall know that I have sent this commandment to you, that My covenant with Levi may continue, says the Lord of hosts. My covenant was with him, one of life and peace, and I gave them to him that he might fear Me; So he feared Me and was reverent before My name. The law of truth was in his mouth, and injustice was not found on his lips. He walked with Me in peace and equity and turned many away from iniquity. For the lips of a priest should keep knowledge, and people should seek the law from his mouth; for he is the messenger of the Lord of hosts. But you have departed from the way; you have caused many to stumble at the law. You have corrupted the covenant of Levi, says the Lord of hosts. Therefore I also have made you contemptible and base before all the people, because you have not kept My ways but have shown partiality in the law."

From the above scriptures, we can see that the main difference between the two categories of followers of God is found in verse 6 and verses 8-9. One category speaks the truth, walks in equity, peace, and justice and turns many away from iniquity, but the other has broken God's covenant, departed from the way, shows partiality, and leads people astray,

If you are the type of Christian that shows partiality in anything based on your selfish personal interest, you should just repent. The Bible says in Isaiah 5:20-25,

> *"Woe to those who call evil good, and good evil; who put darkness for light, and light for darkness; who put bitter for sweet and sweet for bitter! Woe to those who are wise in their own eyes, and prudent in their own sight! Woe to men mighty at drinking wine, woe to men valiant for mixing intoxicating drink, who justify the wicked for a bribe, and take away justice from the righteous man! Therefore as the fire devours the stubble, and the flame consumes the chaff, so their root will be as rottenness, and their blossom will ascend like dust; because they have rejected the law of the Lord of hosts, and despised the word of the Holy One of Israel. Therefore the anger of the Lord is aroused against His people; He has stretched out His hand against them and stricken them, and the hills trembled. Their carcasses were as refuse in the midst of the streets.*

In 3 John 4, the Bible records,

> *"I have no greater joy than to hear that my children walk in truth."*

Therefore, whoever wants to give God the highest joy, MUST of a necessity walk in the truth.

by being like-minded, having the same love, being of one accord, of one mind. Let nothing be done through selfish ambition or conceit, but in lowliness of mind let each esteem others better than himself. Let each of you look out not only for his own interests but also for the interests of others. Let this mind be in you which was in also in Christ Jesus, who being in the form of God, did not consider it robbery to be equal with God, but made Himself of no reputation, taking the form of a bondservant, and coming in the likeness of men. And being found in appearance as a man, He humbled Himself and became obedient to the point of death, even the death of the cross. Therefore God also has exalted Him and given Him the name that is above every name."

So many people started well but somewhere along the line have turned into something else that is far from the example of Christ.

In his Epistle to the Corinthians, the Apostle Paul warns every believer to be watchful (1 Corinthians 3:9-21):

"For we are God's fellow workers; you are God's field; you are God's building. According to the grace of God which was given to me, as a wise master builder, I have laid the foundation, and another builds on it. But let each one take heed how he builds on it. For no

other foundation can anyone lay than that which is laid, which is Jesus Christ. Now if anyone builds on this foundation with gold, silver, precious stones, wood, hay, straw, each one's work will become clear; for the Day will declare it, because it will be revealed by fire; and the fire will test each one's work of what sort it is. If any one's work which he has built on it endures, he will receive a reward. If anyone's work is burned, he will suffer loss; but he himself will be saved, yet so as through fire. Do you not know that you are the temple of God and that the Spirit of God dwells in you? If anyone defiles the temple of God, God will destroy him. For the temple of God is holy, which temple you are. Let no one deceive himself. If anyone among you seems to be wise in this age, let him become a fool that he may become wise. For the wisdom of this world is foolishness with God. For it is written, "He catches the wise in their own craftiness, and again, "The Lord knows the thoughts of the wise, that they are futile." Therefore let no man boast in men. For all things are yours."

If anyone claims to follow Christ and ends up not receiving a reward for following Him, what does that say of the person? In Mark 10:28-31 it is written

"Then Peter began to say to Him (Jesus), "See, we have left all and followed You."So Jesus

answered and said, "Assuredly, I say to you, there is no one who has left house or brothers or sisters or father or mother or wife or husband or lands, for My sake and the gospel's, who shall not receive a hundredfold now in this time—houses and brothers and sisters and mothers and children and lands, with persecutions—and in the age to come, eternal life. But many who are first will be the last and the last first.""

What is the point of running a race without the prize in focus? Zechariah 7:7-10 (MSG) says,

"There is nothing new to say on the subject. Don't you still have the message of the earlier prophets from the time when Jerusalem was still a thriving, bustling city and the outlying countryside, the Negev and Shephelah, was populated? This is the message that God gave Zechariah. Well, the message hasn't changed. God of the Angel Armies said then and says now: "Treat one another justly. Love your neighbours. Be compassionate with each other. Don't take advantage of widows, orphans, visitors, and the poor. Don't plot and scheme against one another—that's evil."

Brethren, the message has not changed. It is man who changes. God never changes (Malachi 3:6). He is the same yesterday, today and forever (Hebrews 13:8).

CHOOSE RIGHT

It does not matter how one looks at it, action and reaction are always equal and opposite. There is nothing anyone will do that will not leave a repercussion.

Galatians 6:7 says,

> *"Do not be deceived, for God cannot be mocked; whatever seed a man does that too he will reap. If you sow love, you will reap a harvest of love, and if one does wickedness, they will also reap the harvest of wickedness."*

A saying of the wise is that whoever brings ant-infested-firewood into the house has just invited lizards to his home.

The truth is that, only he whose conscience is seared can do things that will live an indelible mark on him.

What is it you are doing that your inner man tells you will produce thorns in future?

It is like choosing to answer or to ignore Jesus's invitation of "Come to Me all you who labour and are heavy laden and I will give you rest."

Those who accept the invitation become God's children while those who refuse or ignore the invitation are damned eternally. That is the consequence of such a decision or choice. God cannot lower His standard for anyone even though His grace endures forever.

Make your choice today. Obey God and choose life and life in abundance.

I would like to end with this from Ezekiel 13:1-23:

Judgment against False Prophets

Then this message came to me from the LORD: ² "Son of man, prophesy against the false prophets of Israel who are inventing their own prophecies. Say to them, 'Listen to the word of the LORD. ³ This is what the Sovereign LORD says: What sorrow awaits the false prophets who are following their own imaginations and have seen nothing at all!' ⁴ "O people of Israel, these prophets of yours are like jackals digging in the ruins.⁵ They have done nothing to repair the breaks in the walls around the nation. They have not helped it to stand firm in battle on the day of the LORD. ⁶ Instead, they have told lies and made false predictions. They say, 'This message is from the LORD,' even though the LORD never sent them. And yet they expect him to fulfill their prophecies! ⁷ Can your visions be anything but false if you claim, 'This message is from the LORD,' when I have not even spoken to you? "Therefore this is what the Sovereign LORD says: Because what you say is false and your visions are a lie, I will stand against you, says the Sovereign LORD. ⁹ I will raise my fist against all the prophets who see false visions and make lying predictions, and they will be banished from the community of Israel. I will blot their names from Israel's record books, and they will never again set foot in their own land. Then you will know that I am the Sovereign LORD. ¹⁰ "This will happen because these evil prophets deceive my people by saying, 'All is peaceful' when there is no peace at all! It's as if the people have built a flimsy wall, and these prophets are trying to reinforce it by covering it with whitewash! ¹¹ Tell these whitewashers that their wall will soon fall down. A heavy rainstorm will undermine it; great hailstones and mighty winds will knock it down. ¹² And when the wall falls, the people will cry out, 'What happened to your whitewash?' ¹³ "Therefore, this is what the Sovereign LORD says: I will sweep away your whitewashed wall with a storm of indignation, with a great flood of anger, and with hailstones of fury. ¹⁴ I will break down your wall right to its foundation, and when it falls, it will crush you. Then you will know that I am the LORD. ¹⁵ At last my anger against the wall and those who covered it with whitewash will be satisfied. Then I will say to you: 'The wall and those who whitewashed it are both gone. ¹⁶ They were lying prophets who claimed peace would come to Jerusalem when there was no peace. I, the Sovereign LORD, have spoken!'

Judgment against False Women Prophets

¹⁷ "Now, son of man, speak out against the women who prophesy from their own imaginations. ¹⁸ This is what the Sovereign LORD says: What sorrow awaits you women who are ensnaring the souls of my people, young and old alike. You tie magic charms on their wrists and furnish them with magic veils. Do you think you can trap others without bringing destruction on yourselves? ¹⁹ You bring shame on me among my people for a few handfuls of barley or a piece of bread. By lying to my people who love to listen to lies, you kill those who should not die, and you promise life to those who should not live. ²⁰ "This is what the Sovereign LORD says: I am against all your magic charms, which you use to ensnare my people like birds. I will tear them from your arms, setting my people free like birds set free from a cage. ²¹ I will tear off the magic veils and save my people from your grasp. They will no longer be your victims. Then you will know that I am the LORD. ²² You have discouraged the righteous with your lies, but I didn't want them to be sad. And you have encouraged the wicked by promising them life, even though they continue in their sins. [23] *Because of all this, you will no longer talk of seeing visions that you never saw, nor will you make predictions. For I will rescue my people from your grasp. Then you will know that I am the LORD."*

Young people, my advice to you is that you make the right decision based on God's word so you don't end up making the mistakes I made.

To Ministers of the Gospel, I appeal to you to preach from God's word and not from your own imaginations, so that you don't lose your reward at last.

Thank you for reading.

Evangelist Solution can be reached by:

Email: solutionministries2001@yahoo.com
Telephone: +447889080268

OTHER BOOK BY LAWRENCE OJI

1. From Prison To Pulpit

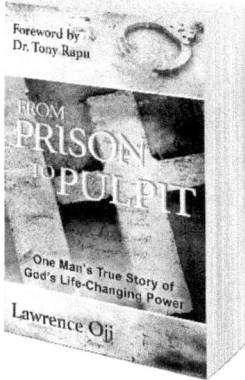

Lawrence (Solution) Oji was a drug addict and jailbird for several years until the saving power of our Lord Jesus Christ touched him inside a prison cell in Italy and literarily "dry cleaned" him and took him away from the squalor of drugs and prisons and placed him on the pulpit. It is an account of how he has come to discover for himself that with God, nothing shall be impossible. In his own words, "There is no life battered, shattered and scattered that Jesus Christ cannot gather again." It is a book recommended for anyone who is challenged by the merciless power of any form of addiction and is in high demand.

Lawrence has ministered in prisons as well as in drug joints wherever he travels to. Read it and see our God in action even today.

ISBN-13: 9788897896968

2. Soul Winning Made Simple

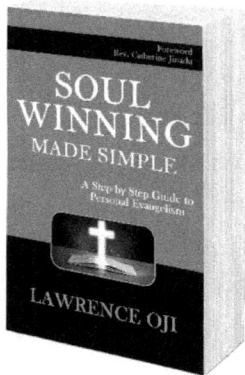

The last words of a dying man in every culture is always taken seriously and to the letter by his loved ones. Jesus's final words were "Go into all the world and preach the gospel to every creature."

Soul Winning Made Simple, takes the reader through a simple step by step method to fulfil this Great Commission by the Master. As you read through, your passion for evangelism will appreciate and the Holy Spirit will reveal to you how much this dying world needs Jesus (John 12:20-21, AMP).

ISBN: 9781907734083

www.ingramcontent.com/pod-product-compliance
Lightning Source LLC
LaVergne TN
LVHW051629080426
835511LV00016B/2253